THE
ENTREPRENEUR'S PLAYBOOK

THE

ENTREPRENEUR'S PLAYBOOK

MORE THAN 100 PROVEN STRATEGIES,
TIPS, AND TECHNIQUES TO BUILD A
RADICALLY SUCCESSFUL BUSINESS

LEONARD C. GREEN
with PAUL B. BROWN

AMACOM
AMERICAN MANAGEMENT ASSOCIATION
New York • Atlanta • Brussels • Chicago • Mexico City • San Francisco
Shanghai • Tokyo • Toronto • Washington, D.C.

Bulk discounts available. For details visit:
www.amacombooks.org/go/specialsales
Or contact special sales:
Phone: 800-250-5308
Email: specialsls@amanet.org
View all the AMACOM titles at: www.amacombooks.org

American Management Association: www.amanet.org
This publication is designed to provide accurate and authoritative information in regard to the subject matter covered. It is sold with the understanding that the publisher is not engaged in rendering legal, accounting, or other
professional service. If legal advice or other expert assistance is required, the
services of a competent professional person should be sought.

LIBRARY OF CONGRESS CATALOGING-IN-PUBLICATION DATA
Names: Green, Leonard C., author. | Brown, Paul B., author.
Title: The entrepreneur's playbook : more than 100 proven strategies, tips, and
techniques to build a radically successful business / by Leonard C. Green, with
Paul B. Brown.
Description: New York, NY : AMACOM, [2017] | Includes bibliographical
references and index.
Identifiers: LCCN 2016042383 (print) | LCCN 2016056943 (ebook) |
ISBN 9780814438176 (hardcover : alk. paper) | ISBN 9780814438183 (eBook)
Subjects: LCSH: New business enterprises. | Entrepreneurship. | Business
planning. | Success in business.Classification: LCC HD62.5 .G728 2017 (print) |
LCC HD62.5 (ebook) | DDC   658.4/012—dc23LC record available at
https://lccn.loc.gov/2016042383

10 9 8 7 6 5 4 3 2 1

Contents

A special offer

Want my feedback (for free)?

The problem I have always had with books on entre-preneurship—and some of them are very good—is that they leave you on your own to get the absolute most out of them. It is solely up to you to understand the author's ideas.

That is not optimal.

And as I said, it is a problem.

Well, at its heart, this book is about learning how to solve problems by thinking differently than every-one else. And so, I figured it was a good idea to prac-tice what I preach (and teach).

If you go to greenco.com you will have the oppor-tunity to be a "virtual" student of mine. You can re-ceive my feedback to every exercise within each chapter.

Visit the website now to learn more.

A quick word before we begin

Just about everyone knows what entrepreneurs do. They solve needs in new (and profitable) ways.

It's how they do it that people rarely understand completely.

In other words, most people get the big picture—what is traditionally referred to as strategy; it is at the tactical level that they fall down.

And so that's where we are going to spend our time: on the tactics and principles that successful entrepreneurs use. That's why I have organized the book by principles, not chapters.

With that by way of background, let's get started.

Find a Marketplace Challenge That Needs to Be Solved or Improved

It's typical in the nation's colleges and business schools for the students to rank their professors. (I've been fortunate. At Babson, the nation's leading college for the study of entrepreneurship, I usually come in at or near the top of the students' lists.)

But it is also typical for professors to rank their students. (It isn't published anywhere, but rest assured, we keep track.)

So, what do my rankings reveal? Two big things:

1. It is easier to teach graduate students than the CEOs who attend my executive education classes. Even though those CEOs are accomplished and learn quickly, the grad students learn faster.

2. And it is easier still to teach undergraduates than all those smart people going for their MBAs.

When I tell people this, they ask the logical follow-up question: "Do you think you would be more effective teaching high school students, compared to those in college?"

My answer? Yes.

Some of them, meaning to be funny, go further and ask, "Does this mean junior high school students would learn even faster than those in high schools, and elementary school students would outperform those in seventh and eighth grade?"

I know they are joking, and even though I had never taught anyone that young, my answer was always (a theoretical) yes.

I will expand more on this point in a minute, but my thinking was simple: the younger you are, the more open you are to new ideas. As we get older, the more we think we know. The problem with that, as Mark Twain pointed out, is clear: "It ain't so much the things we don't know that get us into trouble; it's the things we know that just ain't so."

I knew from teaching that the more open you are to new ideas, the easier it is to be entrepeneurial. And I had always believed that the younger you are, the easier it is to develop the entrepreneurial skills you are going to need going forward. But I didn't know that for sure.

Then, a few years ago, I got my chance to find out.

My grandson, Kenny, was in the fifth grade at the Buckley Country Day School on Long Island, and his class was doing a unit on business and entrepreneurship. Kenny volunteered me to come into his class and talk about what I do.

Kenny's mother, my daughter Beth Green—a lawyer who once worked with the negotiation expert Roger Fisher of *Getting to Yes* fame—was excited but concerned.

"Dad, they're only ten and eleven years old. What can you possibly say to them from your college and graduate school classes that they're going to understand? Buckley wants you to fill ninety minutes. How are you going to hold the kids' attention for an hour and a half?"

Beth then paused and gave me a look that I recognized from her teenage years, the one that conveyed, "You are totally clueless, Dad." But she simply asked, "Are you sure you want to do this?"

I told her it was going to be a piece of cake. I was going to use the same opening-day "presentation" that I give my Babson students.

Beth looked even more horrified, but that is exactly what I did. I stood up in front of Kenny's class and, after we spent a few minutes getting to know each other, I showed them a plain drinking mug and asked what they could do to "alter or change the mug so that it would be worth more." (In business schools, the concept is known as enhancing value. To fifth graders, the idea is described as making more money.)

They got very excited and in minutes came up with the following ideas:

1. Add color.
2. Add designs.
3. Add the name of the school, Buckley.
4. Have two handles.
5. Add a thermometer, to tell you the temperature of the liquid inside.

They passed test number one; they truly enhanced the value of the mug! For my second exercise, I pulled out my smartphone.

"Okay, you all know what this is." (Most had a phone of their own, and they were all very familiar with what the devices could do.)

"Let's do an exercise to see who is most innovative," I said. I divided the class into teams of four and gave them fifteen minutes to answer this question: "It's five years from now: How will you be using your cell phones? I want you to compile a list of as many functions as you can."

You cannot believe what they imagined. Not only would they be able to watch any television program or movie whenever they wanted, everything would be instantly customizable. They would put in their preferences, and shows would be recorded automatically; songs would be compiled instantly into playlists—and everything would be voice activated. Their lists went on and on.

Then, I had them do exactly the same thing that I always have my college, graduate, and even CEO students do during the next part of the exercise. I said, "Now that you have forecasted where the market is going, I want you to think of as many products as you can that people will want to use in the future."

Again, they were remarkable. They produced more ideas faster than any group I have ever taught. In fact, I think one of their ideas is going to make someone a lot of money.

Let me tell you about it.

Say you are about to go shopping at a "big-box" store; Target, Home Depot, Best Buy, etc. These stores are so huge—some are three full acres—that it can be difficult to find anything.

As you enter the store, let's say a Super Walmart, which sells everything a typical Walmart does, plus groceries, you receive an email on your phone asking if you would like to download a detailed map of the store and see what is on sale. If you click yes, not only do you get a map complete with a search function (looking for cereal, it's in aisle 22 on the left), but, as you approach the cereal aisle, you are offered a coupon, via your cell phone, for $1 off a box of Cheerios. Linger in front of the lawn mowers for more than ninety seconds and not only will you get a coupon for $100 off any riding mower you buy today, your phone offers to set up a side-by-side comparison of the models you are considering.

It's a wonderful idea and it is definitely feasible. I checked. (It's surprisingly easy to do with existing technology.)

The idea satisfies one of my criteria for success: it creates a win-win situation—actually, a win-win-win in this case. The customer wins because he gains an easier way to navigate the store and receives targeted discounts. The product seller wins because he is able to provide an incentive to an interested customer to get him to buy. And the store wins because it is creating value for its customers (which will probably increases sales).

Someone, I believe, is going to be extremely successful with this idea.

LOOK AT WHAT'S GOING ON

What have we just learned?

Well, first, my grandson and his classmates are smart. And second, it really is easier to teach entrepreneurship to younger people.

Why would these fifth graders come up with more ideas than my college and graduate students—or CEOs typically do in the same amount of time?

There are three reasons, and they are something to keep in mind, if you are older than ten or eleven:

1. The older you are, the more you've seen, so there is a tendency to be skeptical and say, "No, that will never work, because . . ." whenever you—or someone else—comes up with a new concept.

2. Since you are usually worried that you could look foolish when you come up with a new idea and it fails, you stick to the safest suggestions. When you are ten or eleven, you are not cursed with self-doubt.

3. And most important, they were thinking about entrepreneurship in the most effective and productive way. If you want to become more entrepreneurial, come up with a better mousetrap, as those fifth-graders did. Instead of thinking about a new revolutionary idea that isn't in the marketplace, start by improving on something that already exists to solve a real problem people have.

Let me explain.

One of the first things that invariably happens in my Babson class is that when we begin talking about what products or services the students might sell, someone will say, "I have an idea." Well, I am not surprised they do: ideas are remarkably easy to come by.

But you don't want to start with a completely new idea; you want to start with a market need, which is just a fancier way of saying that you want to come up with a better mousetrap.

For a lot of people, that statement is counterintuitive. They ask: Shouldn't you start by coming up with an idea for a product or service that has never existed in any form?

The answer is no.

Here's why.

It's natural, when you are pondering how you can create a product or service, to want to think about coming up with a unique idea. It would just seem to make sense. After all, if you are trying to create something new, why shouldn't you start with something unique?

The reason you shouldn't, is because, it's remarkably inefficient and it's inefficient because ideas are easy to come by.

I will let you prove it to yourself.

Take the next two minutes and write down all the things you'd love to see created, whether or not you would want to have anything to do with creating them. For example, list that jetpack that would allow you to fly to work and the device that will get the dishes from the table to the dishwasher.

Ready, set, go.

If, you are like most people, you came up with at least 10 ideas within those two minutes. (As I said, generating ideas is easy.)

The problem is you can't do much with most of those ideas. Some are not yet feasible; we don't know, yet, how to get those dishes into the dishwasher by themselves. Others are going to take much more money than you can easily lay your hands on; the cost of mass producing jetpacks that allow you to fly is going to be huge. While the vast majority of the ideas you generate are probably intriguing, odds are, you don't have the necessary skills, talents or even interest in making them a reality.

All this explains why you don't want to start with a unique idea. You want to begin by improving a concept that already exists.

There are three specific reasons why.

For one thing, you won't have to spend a lot of time explaining what you have. The Polaroid camera was eventually a huge success but it took a while. They needed to educate the market. Everyone knew what a camera was and could imagine a better one (one that took sharper pictures or was easier to focus) but trying to sell a camera that developed its own film took a lot of explaining. People needed to understand what it was and be convinced that it actually worked.

You can get some of your best ideas from your competitors.

What are they doing well?

What product or service are they offering you can improve upon?

Second, it's a problem if your idea is a solution to no known problem. For example, it's wonderful you want to create a business newspaper better than the *Wall Street Journal*. I'm sure you could find dozens of little things you think you could improve. The fact is, the *Wall Street Journal* is an extremely good business newspaper and the universe is not clamoring for anything better. They think the existing mousetrap—the *Journal*, in this case—is just fine.

Finally, when you start with an idea, you have to go out and find customers. This is no easy task. When you begin with a market need, you already have them. They're the people who are looking for a product or service like yours one that solves a problem they already have.

DO THIS INSTEAD

As we have just seen, instead of trying to create a radically new product or service, it's always easier to start by trying to solve an existing problem. If you go down this route (and I recommend you do), you will probably end up building off something that already exists.

 ## DON'T SPEND TOO MUCH TIME ON PLANNING

Many of my fellow professors at Babson College spend hours teaching students how to create a business plan. I don't spend a minute on it.

It's not that I think planning is a waste of time. I believe it can be extremely valuable. (See our discussion about the best way to conduct a truly effective Strengths, Weaknesses, Opportunities, and Threats [SWOT] analysis in Principle 12.) It's just that having a detailed business plan can give you a false sense of security. If you are overly dependent on it, the first time you encounter something that you didn't expect—which will probably happen on day one—you're going to be at a loss.

Instead of developing a detailed business plan, a far better approach is to do the minimum amount of planning that will get you under way and adjust as you go (depending on what the market tells you).

When I say all this, someone always asks, "But don't I need a detailed business plan to know if I am on to a big opportunity?"

The answer is no.

The easiest way to get confirmation that you're on to a great idea is to explain your concept in a "Rocket Pitch" (some people call it an Elevator Pitch) of thirty seconds or less, and then ask, "Is this something you would invest in?"

If you get some sort of positive response, you may have spotted a real opportunity.

We will be talking more about this in Principle 2.

If you think about it, you'll realize that is exactly what the kid-creators of the mall map app did. Maps have been around forever, and so have coupons. Their idea simply combined the two to solve a problem: finding items to purchase in a big-box store, getting the best deal in the process.

It's tempting to start with a blank piece of paper when you are just beginning to look for ideas.

Don't.

Instead, begin by searching for existing products/services that can be modified to solve a problem or improved.

To put everything we just talked about into context, let me give you four rules to live by.

RULE #1

Investigate what products are in the marketplace and make yours better (faster, more effective, etc.).

 PROOF THIS WORKS

One Sunday morning, Jack Grumet—my neighbor and the founder/owner of Jo Ann's Nut House (which sells cookies, and, indeed nuts)—was driving along a main street in town and saw a long line of customers waiting to buy freshly baked bagels. The bagels came in over a dozen varieties. One of the main ingredients used was New York City water.

Jack introduced this model nationwide and created the Manhattan Bagel Company, which became a New York Stock Exchange-listed company.

RULE #2

When others see problems, you should look for opportunities.

If you're going to satisfy a market need, you have to listen to the market. Sounds obvious, right? But that means you have to evolve if the market tells you to, and that can be difficult. You've spent a lot of time identifying market need X. You raised money, laid out a marketing plan, and figured out exactly what you need to make X a reality. Then all of a sudden, the market says X is not such a good idea, it could be made substantially better, or it wants a variation of the product.

Can you change in that sort of situation?

Stacy Madison did.

PROOF THIS WORKS

Stacy and Mark Andrus thought they were onto something. They lived in New England and on a visit to the West Coast, they noticed lines of people buying food from sidewalk vendors at lunchtime. Pitas and wraps were just becoming hot in the mid-1990s, and they thought if they could sell theirs in the heart of the Boston financial district at lunchtime, they could probably make a decent living.

They were right. On their first day, they quickly sold out. It was clear that they had underestimated demand for their pitas and wraps. When they got the system down, they routinely made and sold a hundred sandwiches an hour. There were always thirty to forty people queued up, but unfortunately some weren't willing to wait—they got out of line and walked away. Also, there was no telling how many people never joined the long line in the first place.

To deal with the problem of long lines and some unhappy customers, every night Stacy and Mark took the extra pita bread; dusted it with cinnamon sugar, or parmesan and garlic; chopped it into chip-sized wedges; and baked it. Then the next day, Mark and Stacy began handing out the chips to the people waiting in line, thanking them for their patience. Soon, customers showed up specifically asking for the crispy, low-fat chips.

This led to selling their pita chips first from the truck and, soon after, in retail stores.

Flash forward ten years. The bad news, Mark and Stacy are divorced. The good news, Stacy's Chips became a $60 million business. At that point, PepsiCo (owner of Frito-Lay) promptly bought it for what is believed to be approximately one times sales, or $60 million, and hired Stacy as a consultant.

EXERCISE 1: STACY'S CHIPS

I do not believe you can learn to swim by just reading a "how-to-swim" book.

I also do not believe you can learn entrepreneurship just

by reading a book. You have to get into the "water" and learn to swim.

So, why not get into the water by answering these questions about the Stacy's Chips case study.

Presented the way I told it in shorthand, it sounds so simple, straightforward, and inevitable.

But ask yourself these questions. The answers will help shape your thinking as you plan to start something new.

1. Would you have focused on sandwiches or snacks? Why?

2. How would you know you would not be able to do both?

3. If you decided to specialize in one, what would you have done with the investment in the other? Shut it down? Spin it off?

4. Money is hard to come by. How would you have marketed either (or both) products?

5. Where would you find a facility to manufacture your product?

6. What would you call the chips and what message would the name send to the consumer?

7. How would you get retailers to sell the chips?

Next step: Go to the book's website and submit your answers for my feedback.

RULE #3

Don't give customers what they say they want, give them what they need.

Steve Jobs, the cofounder of Apple, was a master at this. Walter Isaacson's 700-page biography of Jobs, which is simply called *Steve Jobs*, should be required reading in every entrepreneurship class because it contains many examples of products Jobs created that people didn't know they needed. No one really knew they wanted a new kind of cell phone, or a different kind of way to buy and store music, until Jobs offered them the iPhone and iTunes.

RULE #4

Utilize the Pareto 80/20 rule.

You've probably heard of the 80/20 rule, which is otherwise known as the Pareto Principle, named after Italian economist Vilfredo Pareto. In a business context, the 80/20 principle is pretty simple: approximately 80% of a company's revenue or profit comes directly from 20% of its resources, like product lines, customers, and even people. The principle has been supported by numerous studies all with the same gut-wrenching conclusion: it's true. Here's an example.

 PROOF THIS WORKS

As a teenager, Joe Ventresca toiled alongside his father, a mason, as he worked with brick and stone to construct homes and office buildings. When Joe was fifteen, he began to notice the real estate agents, who arrived at the construction sites well dressed and driving expensive cars. These men and women made a lot more money than his father, and did so without engaging in physical labor.

After college, Joe worked as a realtor and then decided to start his own real estate firm. His new office comprised ten agents, and he quickly learned that the 80/20 rule applied to real estate agents as well. Two of his employees were hard workers, three were okay, and five were just getting by. Not surprisingly, the two hard workers generated 80% of the profits.

Joe was frustrated. He put in long hours, was dedicated to serving his clients, and was committed to becoming the best. He couldn't understand why eight of his ten employees didn't share these traits.

By chance, Joe had a meeting with a real estate agent from a different agency and learned the following techniques that worked for them:

- ▸ Agents who generated a listing got to have their name and phone number on the for sale sign that was put outside the home. People seeing the sign who were interested would call them, and not the real estate main number. (If people called the main number, the listing agent would split the potential commission with the person who handled the call.)

- ▸ Newspaper ads worked the same way. If you signed up a client, your name was listed as the person to contact in the ad.

- ▸ In exchange for paying a management fee and a share of the monthly overhead, the agents kept a maximum portion of their commission.

EXERCISE 2: THE 80/20 RULE

1. What attributes should Joe be looking for in real estate agents to work in this new way of doing business?

2. Could this model work anywhere else?

3. What is going to keep these agents from going out on their own?

4. The standard real estate commission is 6%. Should Joe set his company's to be higher, lower, or remain at 6%?

5. Is the 80/20 rule applicable to your business?

FIVE TAKEAWAYS FROM THIS CHAPTER

1. **Don't begin with an idea.** Start your search by identifying a large market need.

2. **Make sure you are committed to it.** Sure, the idea of mass-produced flying jetpacks is appealing. But if you don't have a technology background, or it's not something you want to devote most of your life to in the near future, it is better to move on to something else. If you're not truly committed to what you are doing, it'll be much more difficult to raise the money you need and find ways to overcome the hurdles you will invariably face.

3. **Make sure you are confident about the opportunity.** There are very few guarantees in life, and the success of a new venture is never going to be listed among them. Still, you want to be as certain as you can be, going into it, that you have identified a significant market need.

4. **Is the market need sustainable?** What can you imagine that might happen to put you out of business? (Changes in technology: The entrance of a far larger competitor determined to steal your sales?) How are you going to protect yourself today to keep that from happening?

5. **What is your contingency plan if the worst happens?**

A Better Mousetrap Is Not Enough

The good news is that you have, or are convinced you can come up with, a product or service that can satisfy a big need in the marketplace, one that will solve a huge problem.

The bad news is that creating a better mousetrap isn't the end of the journey; it's just the beginning.

As we saw with Principle 1, even if you have the proverbial better mousetrap, the world may not beat a path to your door. The cliché is simply not true. You need to figure out a way to tell people what you have, and to position your product or service in a way that'll keep the competition from eating you for lunch (and breakfast and dinner too).

The positioning and developing of your idea is as important as the idea itself.

This is another lesson I learned the hard way. Let me tell you about it.

We were convinced we had come up with a better mousetrap, specifically a better version of Red Bull, the high-energy drink. We had experience in the beverage business, and we understood how to get the product into stores where there was growing shelf space for this kind of product, so, if we gained even a small percentage of it, we could be very successful.

Red Bull is loaded with caffeine and promised it will keep you going. Our product, Mercury Energy Drink, also had caffeine, and it included ribose, which was another source of energy as well. We figured with ribose, and a formula designed to supply the body with carbohydrates and replace fluids and sodium lost during exertion, we could fuse two categories—sports drinks (Gatorade) with an energy drink (Red Bull)—into a new category that we would call "Sports Energy."

As we thought about what it would take to make Mercury successful, we had the following pluses going for us:

1. We knew the beverage industry.
2. The timing was right for a sports energy drink, given the increasing awareness of the importance of working out and remaining hydrated.
3. We had the finances to launch and promote our product.

So why are people still drinking Red Bull and you have never heard of Mercury? It's primarily because of something we did not anticipate. A successful entrenched competitor has the ability to match a new competitor's price, eliminating the competitive advantage that comes with being less expensive. Red Bull began promoting its product with special deals like a buy one, get one (BOGO) free. They were willing to take a hit to their margins to keep from ceding an inch of shelf space to us.

Could we have come up with alternative marketing approaches? Sure, we could have spent large sums of money:

▸ Advertising
▸ Getting celebrities to endorse the product
▸ Paying to gain shelf space near checkout counters in supermarkets and convenience stores

Why didn't we? Well, creating Mercury wasn't our primary business and while it would have been something we would have been proud of, it wouldn't be the end of the world if it never happened. And so we turned our attention to something else (details in a minute.)

The lessons from our Mercury project were clear to us:

1. You must be prepared for your competitor to change its market strategy and pricing in response to how you choose to market your product or service.
2. You must have financial staying power.

3. You must have the will to persevere. (We will talk more about this later as well.)

5-Hour ENERGY did these things, and they were able to compete with Red Bull.

We decided to abandon Mercury and concentrate our energies and financing in developing Blue Buffalo pet food. When Blue Buffalo had its IPO and became a public company on July 22, 2015, we knew we had made the right decision.

MORE PROOF

Let's stay with this concept with an example of what you should do.

Two Babson students, Dinesh Wadhwani and his brother Danny, came up with a wonderful idea for a product: a longer-lasting lightbulb that saved energy and was specifically designed for warehouses and manufacturing plants. It really was superior to anything on the market, and they figured they could sell it for the same price as the competition.

They came to me looking for affirmation that they had a terrific concept and were on their way to success. I told them it was indeed a better mousetrap, but one, I felt, destined to fail in the marketplace.

"You're never going to build a company given the way you have positioned the product," I said. "For one thing, it's going to be very difficult to get customers to switch lightbulb suppliers. They're not going to accept on faith that yours lasts longer. They're going to tell you they are too busy to test it out on their own and it will cost them money to try it.

"For another, the moment you do win a contract, someone may come out with a similar bulb. Yes, I know you have a patent, but I'm here to tell you the competition will find a way to differentiate their product from yours, or simply copy you and wait for you to sue—making money all the while. In either case, they're going to undercut you on price and you won't win another contract."

Not surprisingly, Dinesh and Danny were extremely dejected after I delivered my critique.

"However, there's a way around this problem," I said. "Go to all the plants and factories, explain what you have, and offer to replace their existing bulbs with yours, *for free*.

"You do the work. You physically swap out the bulbs they have with yours—and you don't charge them a thing. How do you make money? Simply ask for a significant percentage of the energy savings! Most companies will go along with that because you'll be lowering their electric bill, at no cost to them, so they're not going to object to sharing the savings."

Dinesh and Danny took my approach, and today Thinklite is a successful company. Dinesh and Danny were featured in 2015 in *Inc.* magazine's 30 Under 30 (extremely successful entrepreneurs, that is).

And they are because they "dug a moat around their product."

How to Build a Moat

The phrase in the subhead above is borrowed from the man who may be the greatest investor who ever lived, Warren Buffett. It's his shorthand way of referring to a business's ability to create and keep a competitive advantage in order to protect profits and market share over the long term.

> "In business, I look for economic castles protected by unbreachable 'moats.'"
>
> —WARREN BUFFET

Let me give you an example of how this works, courtesy of Investopedia. Suppose you have decided to make your fortune by running a lemonade stand. You realize that if you buy your lemons in bulk once a week, instead of every morning, you can reduce costs by 30%, making you able to undercut the prices of competing lemonade stands.

Your low prices lead to an increase in the number of customers buying lemonade from you (and not your competitors). As a result, you see an increase in profits.

It probably wouldn't take very long for your competitors to notice your method and employ it themselves. Therefore, in a short period of time, your large profits would erode, and the local lemonade industry would return to normal (extremely competitive) conditions again.

However, suppose you develop and patent a juicing technology that allows you to get 30% more juice out of a lemon. This would have the same effect of reducing your average cost per glass of lemonade by 30%. This time, your competitors will have no way of duplicating your methods, at least not for the foreseeable future, as they scramble to come up with a juicing technology of their own.

This is the kind of protection—or moat—you want to have for your idea.

Moat Building 201

It's typical in talking about competitive advantage to first define what it is. Many academics would say it is essentially any factor that allows you to make more money than your competitors who are offering a similar product or service—and only then do they discuss ways to protect your edge.

I think that's wrong. If you aren't thinking about how you're going to create a moat around your competitive advantage from the very beginning, you run the very real risk of wasting a lot of time and effort.

If the students who had come up with the better industrial lightbulb hadn't thought about their moat—installing the bulbs for free—they would've gone out in the marketplace and might very well have promptly been undercut on price (and eventually failed).

You need to be thinking about what kind of moat you're going to have to protect your competitive advantage from day one.

You start by asking: How are you different?

It's one of the most fundamental questions in business: How're you going to position your product/service/idea so it'll be successful? Everyone agrees how vitally important positioning is; then they promptly fall off the track. They instantly start rattling off ways they can position their product or service, assuming that the positioning is going to stay the same forever. That's silly. Your positioning may, and probably will, change over the course of your product's life cycle, as competition and economic conditions change.

How you position your product is up to you. That said, the following ideas, which are not meant to be all-inclusive, could help jolt your thinking:

■ **Low-price provider.** This positioning is self-explanatory and extremely dangerous in the long run, unless you plan to become the Walmart of your industry. The problem with taking this approach is that someone else—because she's found how to do what you do only cheaper, or she really doesn't know what her costs are so doesn't charge enough—can always undercut your price.

■ **High-price/high-quality provider.** You are best in class. You can find examples everywhere you look. Gucci, Lamborghini, etc.

■ **Fastest.** Sure, car manufacturers talk about going from zero to sixty all the time, but that isn't the only place where you position your product around speed. You could have the fastest search engine or seeds for the fastest-growing roses if you are selling to growers and home gardeners.

■ **More convenient and user-friendly.** You could provide one-stop shopping as the big-box stores do. The "doc-in-the-box" walk-in medical centers or companies that offer twenty-four-hour access to their order takers and customer service providers are two other examples.

■ **A better experience.** Going to a minor league baseball game can be more entertaining than going to a major league one where you are cut off from the players, and very little happens between innings. At a minor league game, the players are accessible and readily sign autographs; fans often are allowed to run the bases after the game, and there are contests and other activities in between almost every inning. Other examples of this: Home Depot and Lowes may seemingly stock everything, but nothing beats the local hardware store for service and advice.

 PROOF THIS WORKS

When John Gagliardi, a college All-American and All-World USA Team lacrosse player with the Long Island Lizards, decided to go into the lacrosse manufacturing business, he could have sold the same kind of equipment and clothing as his competitors.

Instead, based on being so personally involved in lacrosse, he realized improvements could be made in both equipment and clothing.

He also redesigned the shafts of the sticks, combining titanium and aluminum, to make a stronger, more affordable product for players of all ages.

In addition, he improved the women's equipment based on their needs (not just smaller versions of the men's equipment). On the marketing side, his company took an edgier approach and targeted players in the inner cities and emerging West Coast adoption of the sport instead of going after the traditional East Coast "Prep School" player. These became the building blocks of his very profitable and successful company, Maverick Lacrosse, which he eventually sold to Bauer Hockey.

■ **Transport.** Ideas that work in one place could very well work in another. This is what importing and exporting are all about. And you see this idea in television all the time when producers take a hit show in England and bring it to the United States.

One last point: although your positioning may change, you can only stress one significant attribute at a time. Of course, you would like to go after every potential market simultaneously, but the reality is that you can't; you have limited resources. You need to stress one key attribute.

But can you subsegment that positioning to reach different groups? Sure. You see it all the time. The classic example is soft drinks.

Typically, companies will come out with the basic drink, say a cola. They quickly follow with a version with no sugar for the calorie conscious. And so you get diet cola. But some people who like diet colas don't like caffeine so you get caffeine-free diet cola. And the company expands from there, offerings: cherry cola, vanilla cola, diet cherry cola, diet vanilla cola, and there are the caffeine-free versions on top of that.

FINANCING THE VENTURE

One of the things that surprised me when I began teaching entrepreneurship at Babson was that many students didn't like numbers, or they didn't want to talk about the numbers. They were more interested in marketing and the production aspects of their ideas.

That's a mistake. As I said, I'm opposed to making them do a business plan where they are projecting out five years. The reason is simple: you don't know what's going to happen during those five years. Still, you need to have a good idea of how much money is going to be required to get you started.

My rule of thumb? Figure out how much money you'll need to keep the company going for a year—without any revenues coming in—and then add 30%.

You can say I am being awfully conservative; but based on my experience, I'm not. It's going to take you longer than you think to assemble a team, refine your idea, and get to market. On top of that, it will take more time than you could ever imagine to get paid for your product or service. For example, you're going to send out invoices that say the customer can get a 2% discount if payment is received within thirty days. In many cases, they're going to pay in sixty or ninety days, and still deduct that 2%.

Have you ever hired a plumber to fix a problem?

If you have, you understand perfectly how to budget for getting under way. Everything is going to take longer, and cost more, than you thought. Like a good Boy Scout, you need to be prepared for this.

Plan accordingly.

DEBT OR EQUITY

While most people may not have thought about, or don't want to discuss financing in detail, when it comes to the question of debt versus equity, they'll talk your ears off. Everyone's starting position is that they don't want to give up equity, and if they have to, it should be nonvoting shares, so that they can control whatever happens to their company. They plan to use other people's money for all the funds they need to get their startup under way (while they retain all the voting shares).

Theoretically it's a lovely position to take. Now, let's talk about the real world. Investors who're willing to invest large sums in your idea are going to want to have a say. So, you can take the idea of two classes of stock—one that has voting rights, the other that doesn't or has limited rights—off the table. They'll never go for it.

CASE STUDY: CANYON RANCH

 PROOF THIS WORKS

Because the website of Canyon Ranch, a health-and-wellness resort, gives such a wonderful description of how it came into being, let me quote pieces of it before I ask you some questions that could spur your thinking.

> "Canyon Ranch . . . began with an aha moment. On New Year's Day 1978, Mel Zuckerman, overweight, sedentary, stressed-out, with high blood pressure and a galaxy of other health problems, resolved to lose forty pounds. By March 4, he had gained four.
>
> "Desperate, he fled to a 'fat farm' in California, planning to spend ten days. He ended up staying a month and changing his life forever. There, he met an inspiring fitness expert who had him running a mile and a half within ten days. As a result, Mel realized that he had, within himself, the power to dramatically improve his health and happiness and that he needed to arrange his life so that he could continue along the healthy track he'd found."

That last sentence is key. Where other "fat farms" just concentrated on providing a weight-reducing menu and exercise, Zuckerman added a psychology component—so that people could truly understand why they were overeating and find new ways to think about food. Extremely pleasant surroundings also helped people actually enjoy the experience.

I tell you this in the interest of full disclosure: my wife, Lois, and I are frequent visitors to Canyon Ranch.

I interviewed Mel Zuckerman because I wanted to do a case study on Canyon Ranch for my Babson College class. Mel emphasized that although there are now a number of competitors who have the same concept, he has added new classes in motivation, stress control, and conflict management. Canyon Ranch offers dozens of different exercise classes and many different types of massage. It has expanded its medical and health services, and its food menus are continually updated and improved.

There are now Canyon Ranches in Tucson, Miami Beach, Lennox (Massachusetts), Las Vegas, and Turkey.

I understand his approach. My question for you is: Do you agree with it? After all, the world is full of companies that had a wonderful product but couldn't turn it into a successful business. (Burger Chef, with its flame-broiled hamburgers, was once the second largest hamburger chain, trailing only McDonald's. And what about the DeLorean car, Lionel Trains, and all those millions of radios and televisions made by RCA?) Will Canyon Ranch join that list, or will it stand the test of time?

EXERCISE 3: **CANYON RANCH**

1. How much should you depend on your personal experiences, as Mel did, as you set off to create a better mousetrap?

2. How good a job has Canyon Ranch done in creating a moat around its idea?

3. How far can the company extend the idea? It has added residential communities near some of its facilities and is now offering its programs on cruise ships. Are these good ideas, or a potential dilution of the brand?

4. What other alternatives could it have taken?

5. What steps should it continue to take, and what new innovations should it add, to position itself to be successful in the future?

6. Should corporations hold corporate retreats and boot camps at places like Canyon Ranch so their corporate executives could get the benefit of the Canyon Ranch Wellbeing Program in addition to an executive education program?

   Note: Take a few minutes and get "back into the water." Answer these questions and send them to me on the website to receive my feedback.

As for outsiders putting up all the money, potential investors are going to want to see that you have invested your own money—even if it's "only" money that you borrowed from your family and friends—to get under way. Outside investors are not going to risk their money on someone who is treating the startup like a theoretical exercise. They will want to make sure that you have "skin in the game."

I understand completely the desire to hold on to as much equity in your company as possible, but owning 100% of a very small business may not be as valuable as owning 10% of something huge. What that means is that it's more than okay. In fact, it may be a good idea to dilute your position (selling your stock to others to help the company become dramatically bigger).

One last point if you want to eat your cake and have it, too. Build into your personal compensation package the right to earn a stock bonus if your sales and profits exceed projections. This will help you increase your equity position as you go. Your investors won't mind because if you earn the bonus, it'll mean you made them a lot of money and a smaller percentage of a larger company is a win-win situation for the investor also.

WHERE DO YOU FIND THE FUNDING?

In class, I use the header "family, friends, and fools" to introduce the subject of where to find the money you need to get under way. Clearly, of the three, friends are the easiest to approach. They like you. So they're most likely to listen to your pitch.

If both you and they make sure they don't invest more than they can afford to lose, the process of raising money from them should go smoothly, whether or not your company is ultimately successful. No, you never want to lose money, especially not your friends' money; but if you explain the potential risk up front in detail and the amount of money invested is relatively small for your friends, you probably still will be friends should the venture not work out.

Raising money from family is far more complicated, regardless of the quality of your idea. It's so difficult because of the emotions involved. In fact, I am convinced that the number-one reason people don't become entrepreneurs is because they are scared they're going to fail, and they certainly don't want to fail in front of people they care about.

Failure can be devastating if your family is involved in the financing. If you borrow $100,000 from your parents to get under way and the venture bombs, you might hear something like this at the Thanksgiving table: "Son, could you pass me the mashed potatoes? While you're at it, can you pass me back the $100,000 I loaned you?"

So, how do you ask your family for money?

Very carefully.

Treat it (as much as you can) as an arm's-length business transaction. Invite your parents' accountant or lawyer to the meeting when you're going to ask them for money. The meeting will go much better if you can also bring along people who have already invested with you. It'll be far better if your folks are not the first people you're asking for funding.

THE ROLE OF THE ANGEL INVESTOR

Angel investors are people who provide backing for startups or entrepreneurs, and they usually do it on better terms than you would get from a bank or a venture capitalist. Invariably, you will find them, or they will find you, as you go about searching for funding. A friend, or potential funding source, will refer you, or they will hear about your venture as you go about looking for money.

It's often easier to persuade them to invest because they can remember when they were starting a company themselves and needed money, so they are empathetic. Invariably, these people have made money in a business venture and have sold out and now miss the action. They're willing to back you, in part, because they like you and your idea, and in equal measure, they want to get back in the game, even if it's indirectly by investing in you.

That makes them easier to sell.

The good news, they want to invest the money. The potentially bad news for you, they'll want to feel part of the decision-making process.

This is one of the rare cases where you may actually want to do a business plan, so that your parents and their advisers feel more comfortable.

As part of the condition of the loan or investment, don't be surprised if your parents say something like, "We hope this works out, but if it doesn't, we expect you to do X," with X being joining the family business or "getting a real job."

DON'T FORGET

Now, let me run through—briefly—three areas that people invariably don't pay enough attention to in getting under way.

Product Distribution

I'm not going to go into this in any detail, other than to say that you need to have your plan for distribution completely in place before you open your doors for business. Retailers and wholesalers are only going to stock and support so many products. You must be able to explain, with certainty, why they'll need to carry yours. For example, with some of our businesses, we've used the concept of having the retailer take the product on consignment. They only pay us if the product sells. We also have offered the retailer a higher gross profit than what our competitors offered, as an inducement to give us a try.

Getting Paid

It sounds like the simplest thing in the world. You make a sale, you get paid.

But it's far from simple. What is your plan to collect? If you can't collect as projected, what is your backup plan if you run short of money?

1. Credit line?
2. Factoring? (A factor is an alternative funding source. The factoring firm agrees to pay you the value of your invoices, minus a discount to cover its commission and fees. The factor gives you most of the invoiced amount immediately and the rest when it receives the money from your customers.)
3. Stretching out the payments you are making to your suppliers?
4. Reducing your cash outlays?

When it comes to this, here are two ideas you may not have thought of:

1. Triple-check that you're being as (legally) aggressive as you can with the tax deductions you're taking. This will reduce the taxes you might otherwise pay, which is another way of saying you'll be reducing your expenses and retaining more cash.
2. Bartering: As our story in Principle 3 about how Bob Reiss started the *TV Guide Trivia Game* makes clear, this can be a very effective way to gain funding.

Advertising

There have been thousands of books written on this topic. I just want to raise the subject here to make sure you consider it in detail.

For what it's worth, I'm big on promotion instead of general advertising. I think television, radio, and newspaper advertising—even the Internet—is far too broad and, as a result, in many cases not cost justified.

Promotion, where you're dealing directly with the consumer

you want to reach, by handing out samples, lets you reach your audience with far less waste.

Two other points about advertising:

1. Everyone always immediately jumps to advertising to the end user, which doesn't have to be the case. Working with the wholesalers and distributors for promotion of your products could be more effective. They can decide if they want to promote your products through the use of "specials" or "coupons" or combining your product promotion with "like-kind products."

2. Involve your customers in your product. Have them tell you how they use it on your website. Make it easy for them to make comments and suggestions on how you can improve, and what products you should add. It's the best form of market research there is.

SWEAT THE SMALL STUFF

Everything we just talked about could strike some people as "details." More than one person has said to me that "the details will take care of themselves" if they get their idea right.

I could not disagree more.

My educated guess is that if you did a postmortem on 100 companies who had a better mousetrap but failed, you would find that 75% did not pay sufficient attention to the details.

I began the chapter by saying a better mousetrap is not enough. Let me end the same way: a better mousetrap is not enough.

FOUR TAKEAWAYS FROM PRINCIPLE 2

1. **Remember, everything is possible.** Armed with your better mousetrap, consider each and every possibility to both protect and expand it.

2. **The kings of yore got it right: Build a moat.** You need to know how you are going to protect your better mousetrap from the inevitable competition you are going to face.

3. **Involve your customers in developing your company's future.** What products would they like to see? What features? Ask them about the problems they would like you to solve for them.

4. **Have (a lot) more money than you think you are going to need.** Starting a business is tough. You don't want to make it tougher on yourself by running out of money.

If You Ain't Passionate About Your Idea, No One Else Will Be

"Passion? Why is he talking about passion; it's not a busi-ness subject. It's squishy, emotional, and seems awfully out of place. I don't recall anyone else writing about passion in a business book."

You're right—and they were wrong not to include it.

You need to have overwhelming faith in what you're doing as you try to create something new; you're going to be giving up an awful lot of things as you get your idea up and running. You'll be sacrificing time with your family and you won't be seeing your friends very much. Your engagement in the outside world is going to shrink dramatically and you'll be thinking about your idea from the moment you get up until the second you fall asleep.

You'd better be passionate about it.

When I say things like this, people who are thinking of starting their own company sometimes respond in one of two ways:

"Well, that may have been the way people did it before, but I believe in work–life balance. I'm going to put in fifty or sixty hours a week getting the business up and running and that's it. I'll work smarter, not harder, and that way, I'll have time for everything else."

To which I say, "I hope you pull it off. But I won't be investing in your idea and I don't think any other smart professional will either. You simply can't give your new business the proper amount of attention it requires if you're spending all your time looking at your watch thinking about quitting for the day."

Unless you truly want to make something happen, the odds are, nothing will. Without that desire, nothing occurs. Your life will be filled in other ways.

I would love to tell you that work–life balance is possible; but if you're starting something new, I can't. The new idea will be taking up most of your life; that's just the way it is if you want to be successful. I don't know anyone who has accomplished a lot who has done it any other way. You don't win at anything in life by giving half effort.

The other way people react? They ask, "Aren't you really missing the point when you talk about passion? My desire to make a lot of money is going to be more than sufficient to keep me going."

It probably won't.

For one thing, it can get you off on the wrong foot. You'll be tempted to chase the "hot niche," and the problem with that is two-fold. First, by the time you realize what the hot thing is, it'll probably be starting to cool off. Think of all those people who opened a video store just as Netflix was coming to the forefront, or all those stores that sold nothing but cupcakes that have come and gone.

Secondly, it can get you to enter a field where you have no natural aptitude. Take a look at any of the nation's largest companies that are still being run by their founders—Limited Brands, FedEx, Marriott, etc. You'll find the people at the helm have always had an amazing feel for their industry, even when they were just starting out.

The point is you want to find a market need that plays to your strengths. You'd be extremely hard pressed to find someone who has started a widely successful business in a field that he or she didn't particularly like.

The desire to make money can keep you going, however, if the new idea is a matter of survival. Here's an example.

 **PROOF THIS WORKS**

It was the Sunday morning of Memorial Day weekend and I was going to spend a few hours in the office. The way our company's coffeemaker works is you have to make a full pot, even if you only want a cup. I didn't want to have just one cup and have to throw the rest away, so I figured I would just stop at one of the convenience stores nearby my office and pick up a large coffee. All the stores were closed for the holiday weekend with the exception of one that's always staffed by the owner, an immigrant, or a member of his family.

"You know, you're the only store around here that's open today," I said as I paid for my coffee. "How come?"

"Because we need the money," the owner said. "If we don't work, we don't eat."

If you're in that kind of situation, then the desire to make money will keep you going. But once you have enough to live, money as the sole motivating factor won't be enough. You'll begin to slack off and once you do, you'll start to look for shortcuts, which will invariably result in treating customers less wonderfully than you should.

So, no, the drive for money isn't sufficient to keep you going.

(You can prove that in the negative. If money was a sufficient motivator, then why are so many rich and successful people continuing to work so hard? They already have more than enough. It's the passion that keeps them going. The majority of successful folks don't set out to be rich. They set out to accomplish a long-term goal, and it's the drive to see it through to the end that keeps them going.)

PASSION FROM A DIFFERENT PERSPECTIVE

There's another way of looking at this. On the surface, it seems that there are four questions you might ask yourself before starting any new venture:

1. Is it feasible? Can it be done successfully?

2. Can I do it—that is, is it feasible for me to accomplish?

3. Is it worth doing? Will there be a market for what I want to sell; is there potential to turn a profit; will people appreciate what I'm trying to do? In other words, does it make sense to put in all this effort?

4. Do I want to do it?

The last question is the one that matters: Do you want to create something?

Why? Either the venture is something that you want, or it's something that leads to something you want. If it's neither of these, there's no reason to act or to answer the other three questions. There is simply no way you are going to give it your full effort if your heart isn't in it to some degree.

Once you want to do something, everything gets reframed. The negative emotional response, to all the unknowns you face in trying to create something new, is reduced. The reality hasn't changed. You still don't know what is out there, but you'll find a way around the problem, because you care about what you're trying to do.

> It's extremely important to select a business that satisfies your personal goals, involves the kind of work you like to do, are good at, and fits your lifestyle.

It's pretty easy to prove this.

Situation #1. Let's say you work for a clothing wholesaler and your boss gives you the assignment of figuring out how to sell everything you carry in Eastern Europe.

Here's how these four questions play out:

1. Is it doable? Who knows? You haven't a clue how to set up a distribution and service network in an underdeveloped country.
2. Can you do it? Maybe. Maybe not. You've never done anything like this before.
3. Is it worth doing? Again, this is something you can't answer with certainty. Who knows the size of the market and whether it will be profitable.
4. Do you really want to do it? No, it's the boss's idea and you already have enough to do, thank you.

Situation #2 is exactly the same, but you're the one who wants to sell the clothes there. You're ready to go off on your own and you think this could be an opportunity. (You have a compelling desire to give it a try, in no small part, because your wife's family lives in Croatia.)

What's the likely result in both cases? It isn't a hard question.

In the first scenario, where desire and passion are not part of the equation, you aren't in any hurry to do anything because the situation is so uncertain and unknown. You keep thinking about what you're up against and search for more data. After all, it's better to study carefully and make sure all the bases are covered than to launch, fail, and have everyone say, "You didn't think it through." At best, you'll put it at the very bottom of your "to do" pile.

The presence of desire alters all that. Because you really want to do it, you're much more likely to take a first, small smart step toward solving the challenge. For example, the next time you and your wife are visiting her family, you stop in and see some local distributors and set up an exploratory meeting with the staff of the Minister of Commerce.

Before beginning anything new, ask yourself this: Is this something I really want to do?

If it isn't, you're likely to be happier and more productive spending your time on something else.

Here's one last reason your passion for your idea is so important. Nobody will be committed to what you're doing if they don't see your desire, your belief in your idea, and your willingness to try to accomplish it.

CASE STUDY: THE TV GUIDE TRIVIA GAME

 PROOF THIS WORKS

It was 1983, and Bob Reiss was watching with interest as a board game became all the rage in Canada. Reiss's experience in the industry had taught him this rough rule of thumb: Every sale in Canada would translate to ten in the United States, and since it appeared that Trivial Pursuit was going to be selling 100,000 copies in Canada, this meant two things:

1. It would sell at least a million copies in the US. (His estimate turned out to be low.)

2. It would open a huge niche for other trivia games, and that represented a potential huge opportunity for Reiss, who sold board games in the US.

The good news was that he had spotted an opportunity and the better news was that he quickly decided how to fill it. He would create a TV trivia game.

Making that decision, of course, was not enough. Given the success of Trivial Pursuit, it was clear there were going to be many other companies who would try to ride the trivia wave, and some would probably pick entertainment in general—and maybe even TV in particular—as their theme. What would make his product different? How could he promote it? The big companies could spend millions on advertising and marketing and there would be no way his tiny company could compete.

The obstacles were daunting, but Reiss was passionate about the idea—and passion, as we have seen, can get you over a lot of hurdles.

THE BATTLE PLAN: PARTNER, PARTNER, PARTNER

Instead of going it alone, he began looking for partners. The strongest in the television space at the time was *TV Guide*. He worked hard to establish contacts and got permission to license their name.

The *TV Guide Trivia Game* was born.

The nice thing about the arrangement was, not only did it give Reiss a differentiated product, it also gave him access to free advertising. In exchange for a 10% licensing fee, *TV Guide* agreed to give Reiss five full-page ads in the magazine for free. The magazine's circulation at the time: 18 million readers.

So far, so good.

Creating a game is expensive, and the people who do it well are highly compensated. That was another hurdle, one that Reiss got around by giving the developer a 5% royalty (which decreased to 3% based on volume) in lieu of a fee.

Selling it to retailers is also expensive. Instead of setting up his own sales force, Reiss went with independent reps, who received a 7% commission on each game sold, but no salary. Collecting on sales is always difficult, so Reiss partnered again, this time with a factoring company who would handle collections.

How was he to get the $50,000 he needed to get under way? You guessed it. He partnered again, giving equity to a rich investor in exchange for picking up the startup costs.

Reiss sold 580,000 games at $12.50 wholesale in 1984, his first year. Gross revenues were $7.2 million (more than $32 million today), and his personal take was estimated at somewhere around $1.5 million back then, $6 million today.

EXERCISE 4: **THE TV GUIDE TRIVIA GAME**

1. Would you have entered a "fad" market?

2. What alternative routes to financing could Reiss have taken?

3. Advertising on TV would have been a natural—but costly—route to go. What alternatives, other than what he did, could he have taken?

4. Since Reiss was successful with this game, should he have followed up with a second game or a completely new idea? (FYI: He didn't do either. Why do you think he didn't?)

5. What would you have done?

If you want to read the whole story, the R&R Case Study (named after the company Reiss started to market the game) is still one of the most-read Harvard Business Cases and is available through HBR.org.

EMPOWERMENT

Given how hard it is to create anything and how much passion is required to overcome the inevitable obstacles, the last thing you want to do is get in your own way. But I guarantee you'll be tempted to. Let me explain.

Invariably, people who start companies assign themselves the position of CEO. Understandable, of course. It's their idea. There are many different ways of being a CEO and unfortunately a majority of people gravitate toward the old command-and-control model where the boss's fingerprints can be found on everything.

Can that work? Sure, but there are four problems.

1. The business may never grow bigger than one person (the CEO) can manage effectively.

2. The company can't move quickly. Since everything has to flow through the chief executive, a potential bottleneck is created. People have to wait for the CEO to sign off before they can move ahead. (Invariably, there is a line outside the CEO's office, from morning to night.)

3. They may not get the best ideas out of their people. Once they understand that the company is set up so everything revolves around the CEO, people are not going to take the time to develop their best ideas. "Why should I?" they ask; "The CEO is just going to do what she wants anyway."

4. It is exhausting.

I know that these four points are true, because I used to be a manager who wanted to control everything. People described me—correctly—as a micromanager. It wasn't surprising that I had a difficult time keeping senior people.

What changed me?

Al Mattia, a longtime friend and fellow CPA.

While my CPA firm was growing 10% a year, Al's firm, Amper, Politziner, and Mattia, was growing 25%–30% annually. I asked Al what was the secret of his success. He said he had attended the Harvard Business School Owner/President Management (OPM) program and I should too.

I took his advice and attended Harvard's OPM. The Executive Education classes were designed to give people who own or run companies a different perspective on their jobs.

Just like all great educational experiences, most of my learning took place from my fellow classmates and outside the classroom. The OPM curriculum was set up so that you worked in teams to analyze various case studies that the professors assigned. I found the studies very interesting. In every one, we were asked to figure out a way a company could operate more efficiently or solve a problem they faced. What I found fascinating was the many different ways my teammates approached the case studies.

They were nothing at all like me. (You'll find a short description of the people I was teamed with in the appendix.) Their reasoning was as unique as they were, yet their answers were always as good as—and often better than—mine.

Each used a strategy that provided him or her with a platform to listen to the people who worked for him or her. They also had advisers who consulted with them and encouraged their people to present ideas and take the initiative.

What I came away with from OPM was the unshakeable belief that I needed to have my employees and board of advisers not only voice their opinions but use their brains and skills to solve the problems we faced without having to wait for me. I was keeping them from contributing all they could to help our company grow and improve. I was wasting our most valuable resource, our people, and that had to change. I needed to create an environment where they could do their best work.

This is empowerment. I became a convert on the spot and even more passionate about our business.

When I got back to the office, I held a firm-wide meeting and said, "I want your input. Everyone here knows more about their jobs than I do and I want you to make decisions on your own, without waiting for a meeting."

Not only did morale go up, but sales and earnings did as well.

When I tell this story, people always ask me if I'm worried about employees making mistakes. My answer is, "Not really." For one thing, everyone always makes mistakes. They were making mistakes before they were empowered, and it would be silly to believe they wouldn't make any once they were. As a leader, it is your job to catch them. But an intriguing thing happened: once I started letting people make their own decisions, the number of mistakes went down. When my employees felt I was going to make the final decision anyway, they didn't always fully think through what they were doing. Once the decision was theirs, they weren't only more creative, but more careful. They had a stake in the outcome; and to underscore how important I thought empowerment was, the bonus part of their compensation was directly tied to the ideas they came up with.

Do they have absolute final say over everything? No, I do. I reserve veto power. But I only use it when I think it's clear that their decisions will harm the company.

Here's an example.

One of the things my employees have implemented at The Green Group, a tax, accounting, and consulting firm, are flex hours. You can work where you want and when you want. The caveat is, "Be accessible, get the work done, get in to the office when you have to, and take care of our clients." (Every employee is encouraged to give their clients their cell and home numbers.)

Having a flexible working arrangement works in my firm; our people are happier and more productive in their jobs.

Flextime, in the minds of our staff, quickly morphed into the idea that our office should be closed on Fridays in the summer. I understood the thought. Our office is located off the main highway used by many to travel to the New Jersey Shore. Commuting by car can be pretty challenging on a Friday in the summer, given the beach traffic. But although I understood why they wanted to close the office on Fridays, this was one of the few times I said no. We needed to be open to meet with clients who wanted to meet with us in person.

The employees understood and countered with the idea of having half the staff in the office on Mondays and the other half in on Fridays. This was more than fine with me, as long as the office was staffed at all times.

I am a firm believer in the great benefits of presenting small groups of employees real situations and challenges that need solving, and hearing the amazing ideas they generate.

Will empowerment work for you? I truly believe it will, if you can wrap your mind around giving up control. I know that's no small thing for people who are used to being the smartest person in the room.

We've talked about the advantages to the company if you take this approach; but, before we leave the topic, let's talk about the personal advantages to you as well. If you delegate and empower, it frees you to do the things you like to do and think about where you want to take the company. You don't have time to think like this if you're constantly putting out fires.

For the people still reluctant to empower, why not use the success formula that has worked in so many different situations. Take baby steps. If you want to lose twenty-five pounds, you set a goal of a pound a week. If you want to run a marathon, you start by running a mile the first week and build from there. With empowerment, begin by delegating small things and see how it goes. Let employees make decisions up to $1,000 of expenditures. If you like the results, and I think you will, you can give people more and more responsibility.

SOME DAYS ARE JUST LIKE THAT

I often say that if you love what you're doing, then going to the office isn't work. I truly believe that. If you feel that way, it's easy to keep your energy and passion up.

Does that mean every day is a walk in the park? No.

What gets me down is when I lose. I thought we were going to get a new client, we didn't; I was convinced the new product we had been working on was going to be a smash—it bombed.

When I get discouraged I try to figure out what I did wrong or what I could have done differently. That helps keep me going. You learn from your mistakes and move on, convinced that you will do better next time. We will be talking—in detail—about how you learn from mistakes in Principle 11.

FOUR TAKEAWAYS FROM THIS CHAPTER

1. **If you are not passionate about your idea, you should not be doing it.** You won't give it your best effort.

2. **Conversely . . . if you truly love what you are doing, it isn't work.**

3. **How are you going to run the operation?** My suggestion, experiment with empowerment. You'll get fresh ideas, your company will be able to move faster, and you will be far less stressed.

4. **You are going to make mistakes.** Unfortunately, it is part of the journey. Learn from them, build off of them, and keep going (even harder).

PRINCIPLE 4

*Experiment!**

Even though I spend part of my time teaching, I believe most of the nation's schools have put us at a disadvantage.

The reason is simple. The way we were taught to reason works well if we are facing a predictable future, but not so much in the world as it is now. (No one would say things are getting more predictable.)

The approach we were taught to use to solve problems certainly doesn't work well if you are trying to create anything new. All you have to do to see that is revisit the steps you were taught in planning your future.

You remember the logic you were instructed to follow:

1. You, your parents, teachers, or bosses forecasted how the future would be.
2. You'd construct a number of plans for achieving that future, picking the optimal one.

---

*I am indebted to my former boss, Leonard A. Schlesinger, now the Baker Foundation Professor of Business Administration at the Harvard Business School, for helping to create the foundation for this chapter. When Dr. Schlesinger was president of Babson, he (along with Charles F. Kiefer and Paul B. Brown) wrote a book called *Just Start* that helped me crystallize my thinking when it came to experimentation.

Len, Charlie, and Paul followed that book up with *Own Your Future: How to Think Like an Entrepreneur and Thrive in an Unpredictable Economy*, which they wrote for AMACOM.

The authors were kind enough to give me permission to build on their ideas. In exchange, not only do I want to thank them, but I suggest you look at both books because they are very good.

3. You'd amass all the necessary resources (education, money, etc.) to achieve your plan.

4. You'd go out and make that plan a reality, taking the most direct route.

As I said, when tomorrow is going to be a lot like today, this approach works just fine. But what is a very smart approach in a knowable or predictable future is not smart at all when things can't be predicted, like when you are trying to get a new idea off the ground. All that planning goes right out the window when you hit your first unexpected obstacle—and that is likely to occur on Day 1. (See the discussion on why business plans are pretty much a waste of time in Principle 1.)

All this raises an obvious question: When you are in a situation—such as starting a company, or creating anything new, for that matter—where you can't perfectly plan your way to success, what is the best way to achieve your goals?

Treating an uncertain world as if it were predictable only gets you into trouble.

Fortunately for me, my former boss, Leonard A. Schlesinger, who was president of Babson College, crystallized the best approach to use. It was one that I had been using instinctively, but I didn't recognize that until I read Len's books *Just Start* (Harvard Business Review Press, 2012) and *Own Your Future* (AMACOM, 2014).

Len starts with the premise that the world is probably going to get more unpredictable rather than less, so the ways of thinking that have gotten us where we are today will be insufficient tomorrow. What follows from that is you need a new way of acting, one that complements—not replaces—the way we were taught to think.

(Much will remain predictable, and you don't want to abandon a set of skills that works well in certain situations.)

Len (along with his coauthors Charles F. Kiefer and Paul B. Brown) reduced his idea for dealing with uncertainty—and again, there is nothing more uncertain than trying to create anything new—to a simple formula. You figure out what you want to do and then you:

1. **Act.** By taking a small step toward your goal. After you do, you pause to see what you have learned.
2. **Learn.** You incorporate that learning into how you are thinking about achieving your goal.
3. **Build.** You build off that learning in preparation for taking your next step. Then you repeat the process, which is the last step.
4. **Repeat.** You take another small step; pause to see what you learned from step two; building that learning into what you do next; and then take another small step. And so on.

That cycle continues (i.e., repeats) until you succeed, know you are not going to, or decide there is another, more appealing opportunity to pursue.

> Take action. Embrace uncertainty. Create the future.

In other words, when facing the unknown, you *act* your way into the future you desire, you don't *think* your way into it. Thinking does not change reality, nor does it necessarily lead to any learning. You can think all day about starting a restaurant, but thinking alone does not get you any closer to having one.

ACTION TRUMPS EVERYTHING.
(Here are thirteen reasons why.)

I learned a lot from the former Babson College president Leonard A. Schlesinger's Act. Learn. Build. Repeat. (ALBR) model.

The key part of the model: taking action.

Why is it so important? In their book, Len, Charlie, and Paul gave thirteen reasons:

1. If you act, you will find out what works . . .

2. . . . and what doesn't.

3. If you never act, you will never know what is possible and what is not. You may think you know, but you won't be able to point to anything concrete to prove you are right.

4. If you act, you will find out if you like it . . . with "it" being whatever the new action is.

5. . . . or if you don't.

6. Acting leads to a market reaction, which could point you in another direction. You thought you were going to open the world's best Italian restaurant. Taking a small step toward that goal, you began hosting large dinner parties and cooking for the monthly meeting of the Elks Club to try out your recipes and you discover firsthand what cooking and serving food to strangers is like. It turns out people raved about your cooking, but were surprised you didn't want to talk to them. You, in turn, were left cold by the experience. You hated interacting with people; the idea of doing all the logistics necessary (finding a place, dealing with the constant turnover of servers, etc.) made you break out in a cold sweat, and you really didn't want to prepare more than three kinds of entrees at a time. You learned you liked the cooking part of running a restaurant but weren't crazy about all the rest. Your action—the decision to take steps toward starting a restaurant—caused a market reaction—they loved the food but found you to be a cold fish; you loved the cook-

ing but could do without everything else—that persuaded you to go into high-end catering and hire someone to deal with the clients.

7. As you act, you can find people to come along with you. For example, in talking to your suppliers, you ended up meeting the world's most organized person. She now runs the day-to-day operations of your catering business and is a 10% owner.

8. As you act, you can find ways to do things faster, cheaper, better. You discover, after making your world-famous Chicken Parmigiana fifty times, that you can prepare the dish in eight steps instead of eleven.

9. If you act, you won't spend the rest of your life going "I wonder what would have happened if . . ."

10. If all you do is think, you may end up being less interesting as a person. Who would you rather sit next to on a plane: someone who started a successful rock-climbing store (or even an unsuccessful one), or someone who only thought about it?

11. If all you ever do is think about stuff, you can gain tons of theoretical knowledge, but none from the real world. You become like that woman in the fable who knows the price of everything but the value of nothing. In other words, if all you ever do is think . . . all you do is think.

12. Action always leads to evidence. You act, therefore something changes, and in observing that reaction, you gain knowledge. (Hmm, if I drop an egg from waist height, will it shatter?) Thinking doesn't lead to proof—or messy floors. As Scott Cook, the founder of Intuit, says: "Evidence is better than anyone's intuition."

13. If you act, you know what is real. You always want to know what's real.

You will remember when I started talking about ALBR; I said it all begins with what you really want to do. That's the "passion" part we talked about in Principle 3. Without passion, implementing the model effectively will be substantially harder, and starting anything new is difficult enough without you handicapping yourself.

If you have that passion, then Step 1 is to Act. YOU HAVE TO START! This is what separates entrepreneurs from everyone else—that is, all those people who talk about creating something new but never do.

Starting is scary. Starting means you put yourself—and your money—out there and at risk. Starting means you are facing, head-on, the possibility that you may fail and fail in front of family and friends who may have provided funding. Instead of doing any of those frightening things it is easier, and feels safer, to keep *thinking* about your new idea.

If that is the course you take, you will never start anything.

So, while I understand why you think you have to do a lot of research before you begin, it really isn't necessary—or helpful. Instead, create a prototype or verbally sketch out your idea and ask people on the spot to write you a check for the product or service you plan to provide. If they do, you are on to something.

If they don't, really listen to what they have to say. What is it that they don't like? What would it take to get them to buy? Blue Buffalo started in 2005 with approximately ten products and no test market or focus groups. It got on the shelves and the marketplace decided if it was a good product. (By 2014, there were more than five hundred products and still growing.) This is no small point. You may think you have the greatest idea in the world, but it is only the market that will tell you if you are right. If it tells you that you need to change your product, then you need to change your product.

FOUR TAKEAWAYS FROM THIS CHAPTER

1. **Act.** Nothing happens unless you do.

2. **Learn.** Newton got it right. Every action causes a reaction. Learn from it.

3. **Build.** Build that learning into your plan for achieving your goals.

4. **Repeat.** Keep reinventing yourself. It's very hard for your competition to hit a moving target.

If You Are Not Failing (Occasionally), You Are Not Aiming High Enough

A lot of potential entrepreneurs have trouble with the concept expressed in the chapter title.

Intellectually, they know the path that leads from idea to marketplace is not going to be smooth, and that invariably some of the things they're going to try along the way will not work. But it's that word *failure* that drives them nuts.

They simply don't want to be associated with "failure." So, they get defensive when I say that failure isn't only an integral part to becoming successful, it's often essential. They stop listening and start coming up with all kinds of reasons why I must be wrong.

This puzzled me for a long time until I finally figured out that they were thinking about failures one way, and I viewed them another.

Every time something fairly major went wrong—consumers said they didn't like the prototype; a major distributor they were counting on to carry their product said no—these people considered it a failure.

I wouldn't. I'd call it a "setback," and the difference is more than a matter of semantics. If you can walk away from the disappointment and live to fight another day it is not a failure. To me, a failure is when you're completely wiped out, when you don't have any more resources to try again.

With this by way of background, you understand why I always tell people experiencing what they consider to be a failure that it is okay as long as it does not wipe you out. If you lose all your money on your first attempt, it's going to be extremely hard to get a second turn at bat. People will be reluctant to invest with you, especially if your initial set of investors lost their shirts. On top of that, your confidence will be down. ("I tried something before and it failed. I'm not sure that I want to try again.") That is going to make any subsequent effort more difficult. You're going to be more tentative and move more slowly and quadruple-check everything because you're petrified of making another mistake.

> If you can live to fight another day after a disappointment, it isn't a failure. It's an opportunity to learn and grow—if you take advantage of it. (If you don't, you're right. It was a failure. You wasted time, effort, and money.)

All this underscores two important points.

First, as we talked about in the last chapter, you want to take small steps toward your goal so that you aren't out a lot of money should things not work out. This will allow you to fight another day.

Second, you want to learn from things when they don't work out. Setbacks—small or large—cost you time and money; that's expensive enough. You don't want to add to the problem by failing to learn from it.

IT'S BETTER NOT TO FAIL

Of course, you would prefer not to have setbacks—or, at the very least, limit how many. Let's talk about how to do this, starting with the big misconceptions that many people have. If you ask people to free-associate when you say the word "entrepreneur," invariably they'll come back with some variation of the words *risk–taker*. It's easy to understand why.

1. Starting anything is risky.
2. People who create new ventures, products, and organizations seem to have more nerve than the rest of us.
3. The press tends to portray these men and women as swash-bucklers. There always seems to be this sort of sentence in the media profiles about them: "And just when it looked like Mr./Ms. Entrepreneur was going to fail, they bet everything on one last roll of the dice—and today they have enough money to buy Wyoming."

Well, I admit it makes fascinating reading . . . but it simply isn't true. Successful entrepreneurs are not risk-takers; they're *calculated* risk-takers, as we will talk about in detail in Principle 8.

CALCULATED RISK-TAKER IN ACTION

 ### *PROOF THIS WORKS*

Mike Holland is a Harvard College and Columbia Business School graduate who entered the business world in financial services; some people call what he does wealth management. Along the way, he watched, observed, learned from, and later worked for one of the legends of Wall Street, Saul Steinberg.

After a discussion we had one day, Mike decided to go from being a well-paid executive with Steinberg to starting Holland Company. Starting his own company would be a calculated risk with no guarantee that he would match the salary he had been earning.

The company prospered. Mike's strategy was to invest for the long run in quality companies with great management. The stock market fluctuates, but Mike sticks to his strategy and consistently outperforms both his peers and the Standard & Poor's.

Mike is a regular guest on CNBC and Bloomberg and is a trusted adviser to many funds. Would this have happened if he had not taken the calculated risk of going out on his own?

WARNING: THIS INVESTMENT MAY FAIL

I'm amazed at how many people don't tell those who're going to invest in their idea that it may fail.

I understand why you wouldn't want to.

For one thing, you don't expect it will. After all, you wouldn't be entering into the venture if you thought success was unlikely.

For another, telling people up front and in writing that what you're about to try might fail gives them a legitimate reason not to invest in you.

Still, it's not only the right thing to do, it also makes strategic sense. Investors will be slightly less unhappy if they have been warned and the venture fails. Because you warned them in detail, you'll be able to go back to them to try to gain funding for a second venture saying, "I think we will get it right this time."

It also makes sense because it serves as a defense if the venture fails and the investor decides to sue you.

As much as you don't want to, warn your investors up front and in writing.

GUARD AGAINST FAILURE
BY NOT BUYING A FRANCHISE

Despite our best intentions, sometimes we make really bad decisions. Take buying a franchise, which many people see as a way to minimize the risks of entrepreneurship.

Now, I know some people don't think franchisees are entrepreneurs. But those people are wrong. Franchisees are entrepreneurs by definition. The dictionary defines an entrepreneur as "a person who organizes and manages any enterprise, especially a business, usually with considerable initiative and risk."

But you don't need a dictionary. Just common sense. In the for-profit world, an entrepreneur is someone who creates and runs a new business where one did not exist before. No, the Subway franchisee didn't create Subway. But she certainly created a Subway where there never was one before.

But they don't take much risk, you cry, and the dictionary definition said that risk is part of being an entrepreneur.

Well, there are two answers to that. First, as we mentioned briefly in the beginning of this chapter, and will talk about in more detail later on in the book, most successful entrepreneurs do everything in their power to minimize risk. The best ones are the most risk-adverse people on earth. They don't like risk. They accept it as part of the game and then work extremely hard to reduce it to a minimum.

And that brings us to the second point—the one about making a bad decision and increasing our chances of failure. It turns out that buying a franchise is more risky than you might think.

How can that be, some people ask me. The franchisor has proven to be successful—otherwise she wouldn't have a franchise to sell, people who don't think this through assume. The franchise has a proven way of running operations, one that she's going to give you to follow, and then she promises to provide you with help to get under way.

What could possibly go wrong?

A lot.

The U.S. Small Business Administration compiles a franchise failure list each year, and invariably the percentage of failures among some franchisors tops 50%, meaning more than one of their two franchises fails.

Buying a franchise is no guarantee against failure.

CASE STUDY: COLUMBIA RESTAURANTS

PROOF THIS WORKS

It is hard to imagine today, since Columbia Restaurants are being run by the fifth generation, and the family's collection of seven establishments on the west coast of Florida are the most popular they've ever been, that there was a moment when there was a very real chance that the restaurant could go out of business.

It happened back in the 1930s, when Columbia was nothing more than one small family restaurant in Tampa. Things were tough for business everywhere during the Depression, and Columbia was no exception. But Casimiro Hernandez, Jr., the second-generation owner, was convinced that he had an idea that could save the restaurant.

He would build the first air-conditioned dining room in Tampa, complete with an elevated dance floor. The new, unique facility would be a perfect place for all the big bands, which were dominating the music scene, to play.

There was, however, an obvious problem. He didn't have the tens of thousands of dollars he needed to finance the construction, and there was no way anyone would lend him the money. There were just insufficient assets to back a loan, and his sales were only approximately $100 a week.

Casimiro went to his local bank and asked for the equivalent of what today would be a $350,000 loan. Not surprisingly, they turned him down.

So then Casimiro began to think of what, today, we would call a win-win proposal.

"I understand why you said no," Casimiro said to bank officials, "but if you finance us, I'll put a prominent sign in the restaurant saying that you made the loan and you're a friend to the Cuban people. That will help you in the community and differentiate your bank from all the others. Also, we'll never forget you, and you'll be our bank for as long as we're in business."

His argument carried the day. In 1937, Columbia opened the

Patio Dining Room, which the company's website says "resembled a courtyard, like the ones found in Andalusia in the South of Spain, surrounded by a balcony with a colorful mosaic-tiled fountain in the middle. A retractable glass skylight was installed, giving the room a wonderful bright and sunny look during the day and an enchanting glow at night."

Creating a win-win situation for the banker made all the difference.

(We will be revisiting Columbia Restaurants to make another point later on.)

EXERCISE 5: COLUMBIA RESTAURANTS

1. When someone first says no to you, what's your first reaction?

2. What should it be?

3. Even before asking for something (the sale, the contract, a loan), are you thinking about the way you can present it so it's in their best interests, or are you only thinking about your interests?

4. Do you understand what a win-win scenario is?

THERE IS AN UPSIDE TO FAILURE

I know the words above are true, because this is what I have experienced myself; the stress brought about by adverse business conditions makes you work harder and smarter. It makes you much more focused than any number of successes.

Very few people doubt the truth of this, but they push back in a different way.

"Who needs the stress," they say. "Stress is not something to look forward to, no matter how positively you paint the picture. I want things to go smoothly."

We all do, but it won't happen. So you need to accept that fact going in. Besides, if you won every game you played, eventually you would stop trying as hard. You'd take bigger risks because you were bored, and you would begin to get cocky. Stress will keep you focused on the fundamentals of what made you a success in the first place.

ANOTHER WAY TO LOOK AT FAILURE

This is a business book. But allow me a brief personal aside to show you that what we have been talking about can apply to your personal life as well.

When I was in my forties, I decided that one of the few athletic events I could still do well in was running. So, I set goals to run in 5K races, then 10K races, half marathons, and finally full marathons. I ran in the Boston Marathon (Charity Division) three times.

Then I was diagnosed with non-Hodgkin's lymphoma and I stopped running for a few years. When the doctor said I was sufficiently recovered, with the help of the Babson Track Coach, Russ Brennen, I once again set running a marathon as my goal.

This time, I chose the Boston Marathon Jimmy Fund Walk, which raises money for the Dana-Farber Cancer Institute. They use the Boston Marathon trail—26.2 miles including Heartbreak Hill, and at first I was disappointed because I could only do a half marathon.

When I realized it was not a defeat, it would be a victory to accomplish that, I started to enjoy the experience. I stopped at rest stops and talked to fellow runners/walkers, many of whom were either recovering from cancer or raising money in memory of someone who had lost his or her battle.

It put a different perspective on my life; and then, after that, I went on to complete several full marathons.

The biggest failure is . . .

NOT starting. People can be extremely risk averse, and the idea of the venture not working out can scare them to the point where they never get under way.

They keep thinking about the idea and/or maybe doing more and more research, and they never pull the trigger.

They take too long to test the market, putting off actually beginning, to the point where the competition has passed them by.

All these situations are sad.

As we've said before, if you think you have a good idea, get into the marketplace as quickly as you can and see what happens. Who knows, you might become Mike Holland.

LEARNING FROM "FAILURE"

Let's bring together everything we have talked about in the chapter here. Consider these two failures:

1. Ignighter was just another dating website, struggling to compete with all the other similar companies out there. They stepped back and began to examine the clientele to see if there were any patterns. They noticed that a lot of their clients were from India.

"Hence, we did what was sensible," the company's website notes. "We launched operations from the incredibly warm and just as fast-paced Mumbai. A re-brand that made us better and more suitable for our Indian audience soon followed and Ignighter became StepOut. Today, we're one of the fastest-growing websites in India."

2. Back in the 1990s, Target was seen as just one more discounter, a slightly nicer version of Walmart or Kmart. It was not a success. By entering into deals with designers such as Isaac Mizrahi and Michael Graves, who provided the store with "pared-down" versions of their offerings, the company differentiated itself and became successful.

You could say the initial efforts of both Ignighter and Target were failures—after all, neither one gained a lot of traction. But by learning from what did not work—what the uninitiated would call a failure—they were actually laying the foundation for success.

CALLING ON A HIGHER POWER

I recognize that the Pew Religious Landscape survey recently reported that about 23% of the U.S. population is religiously unaffiliated, atheists, or agnostics. And I never talk about religion or faith until someone else brings it up. If they do, especially if they're going through a tough time and feel that they have been singled out unfairly, I might give them a copy of the prayer below. It helps me keep everything in perspective.

Specifically, it provides me with two important reminders.

1. When things don't go well, you can complain, or you can say, "Okay, I've been given a challenge; what am I going to do about it?"
2. It reminds me that the Lord won't throw anything at me that I cannot handle.

This prayer has helped me a lot. I put it here not to proselytize, but to help you get through tough times as well.

Dear Lord,
Help me to be a sport in this little game of life.
I don't ask for an easy place in the lineup—play me anywhere you need me. I only ask for the stuff to give You 100% of what I've got; and when the tough breaks seem to come my way, I thank You for the compliment.
Help me to remember that You won't ever let anything come my way that You and I together can't handle.
Help me to take bad breaks as part of the game. Help me to understand that the game is full of hard knocks and trouble

and make me be thankful for them. Help me to appreciate that the harder they are, the better I like it.

And Lord, help me to always play on the square, no matter what the other players do. And if the great players who have lived have found that the best part of the game is helping other guys who are out of luck, help me to find it out too. Help me to be a regular fellow with the other players. Help me to remember the importance of family.

Finally, Lord, if fate seems to uppercut me with both hands and I get laid on the shelf in sickness, old age, or misfortune, help me to take that as part of the game also. And help me not to whimper or squeal that the game was a frame-up or that I had a raw deal.

And when, in the falling dusk, I get the final bell, I ask for no lying tombstones. I'd only like to know that You feel that I have done everything to the best of my ability.

Finally, when You, the great scorer, come to tally up my life, I want you to write it is not whether I won or lost—but how I played the game.

I mentioned Columbia Restaurants earlier. Richard Gonzmart, the fifth-generation family owner and one of the best entrepreneurs I have ever met, wrote these moving words to me after I called him when I found out he had prostate cancer:

We each face a time in our life when we have faced defeat, losing or not accomplishing a goal. It is how we address this situation that matters. Giving up is never an option for me.

In sports, you give your all until the last second ticks off the clock; in running you continue on until you cross the finish line, even if it means having to walk or even crawl. In business, we face challenges, but most important is preserving our integrity, the belief in our work and mission. In marriage, it is maintaining respect and sharing our love with our spouse and children.

My faith helps me in the many challenges I have known and know today in life; the courage to see that tomorrow holds another opportunity to succeed is what keeps me going. To give up is to lose our belief and faith; our heart is the engine, the life blood of who we are, what we are today and tomorrow and beyond.

Here's to life and embracing each day with gratitude, passion, compassion, kindness, patience, integrity, faith, peace, and purpose.

I will let an unlikely source add a coda to that.

Howard Cosell became a legend as a sportscaster and TV celebrity, and one day, my friend Josh Mayberry, who worked at ABC, introduced Howard to me. Howard autographed my copy of his book with the following inscription: "The ultimate victory in competition is derived from the inner satisfaction of knowing that you have done the best you are capable of and have gotten the most out of it."

FOUR TAKEAWAYS FROM THIS CHAPTER

1. **Recognize the risks.** One way to keep failures to a minimum is by remembering that entrepreneurs are not risk-takers; they're calculated risk-takers.

2. **Handle problems as they arise.** There is a huge difference between a setback, an obstacle that you need to get around, and a failure where you lose all your money.

3. **Remember, it ain't over till it's over.** How many great teams are losing at halftime, make adjustments, and come back to win the game? For example, quarterback Andrew Luck threw four sec-

ond-half touchdown passes and scored on a fumble recovery, leading the Indianapolis Colts from a four-touchdown deficit to a historic 45–44 comeback victory over the Kansas City Chiefs in a wild-card game in early 2014. Keep that in mind, when you encounter an obstacle—and adjust.

4. **Don't view stress as a bad thing.** Sure, we all want things to go smoothly all the time, and when they don't, it causes stress. But stress keeps you remarkably focused on solving the problem at hand.

Work Hard

(You'll Be Amazed at

How Many People Don't)

I had a scheduled meeting at a client's office for 9:00 A.M., and as I pulled into their parking lot at 8:52 I was surprised at the number of people who were sitting in their cars. Some were reading the newspaper or talking on their cell phones. Others were just sitting there staring into space.

I walked slowly to the front door, looking back at the parking lot every few seconds since I hadn't a clue what was going on.

At 8:58, it looked as if all those people in the parking lot received a signal only they could hear. They all stopped what they were doing, got out of their cars, and headed into the building. They were employees of the firm and they were going to be at their desks at 9:00 A.M.—when the workday started—and not one minute before.

My meeting ended just after lunch, so I wasn't there at 5:00 P.M.; but I will guess they were all back in their cars by 5:02, and not going to work one minute more than they had to.

Unfortunately, I can't say that I was surprised.

You would think that hard work would be taken as a given. It's not. In fact, I think you can tie it directly to the 80/20 rule we talked about in Principle 1. The top 20% of employees do 80% of your work; 20% of your team produces 80% of the profit and 80% of the new ideas.

Now, I am not denigrating the 80%. I never expect people to put in the hours I do, but I do expect them to give the same effort during the time they work. If they don't, I'll suggest—in no uncertain terms—that they would be happier being employed elsewhere.

Why would you tolerate the 80%? Well, you wouldn't in the early days of a startup when you have just a handful of employees, and they *all* need to be dedicated to the concept you're trying to create. You should only have 20-percenters in the room.

But as the company grows, those 20-percenters need people to do the "support" work, the tasks that can be scheduled between 9 and 5, or whenever office hours are. People in IT, the accounts-payable department, lawyers, and the like. Besides, I understand that for some people, work is not at the center of their lives. They're passionate about painting, saving stray animals, or getting their rock band off the ground. Traditional work is just a way for them to fund the things they really care about. As long as people give me maximum effort at work, I respect that their true passions lie elsewhere.

There are two points to make about this. If you're one of these 80% people, you need to know your chances of advancement in any firm are limited. (That just makes sense. Why would anyone promote you when the person next to you is more committed to what the company is doing and putting in more hours?)

MOTIVATING THE OTHER 80%

I said having 80% of your workforce only doing 20% of the work is okay if you are getting maximum effort out of that 80%.

So, how do you do that?

The onus is on you, the leader. You need to get them to be part of your team and involved and wanting to do something greater than themselves, and/or have them wanting to perform better than they ever have before. You have to make them understand that nothing great was ever produced by being lackadaisical.

Think about the best leaders of all time, whether they were in sports, John Wooden at UCLA; the military, George S. Patton; or business, Herb Kelleher. They each got people to achieve more than they ever thought they could.

I know that is my goal, whether I am leading a company or teaching. I tell my students at Babson that my classes will end up being the most demanding they have ever had, but I promise them that the hard work will be worth it. They'll probably end up leaving with an idea that will lead to a successful business.

I'm serious about the hard work. For my 8:00 A.M. class, we lock the classroom doors precisely at 8. Other professors may let you come in late, but I don't. (If you try to sneak in the back door, your classmates will boo you.)

Typically, at Babson, a student will spend as much time on homework as he or she does in class. If the class is three hours long, homework takes three hours. For my courses, the homework portion could be double or triple the class time. Whatever it takes to come up with the best out-of-the-box solution is the time you need to spend on the case study we're examining, because 75% of your grade is based on your answer to the questions posed in the case.

To persuade my students to do all that work, I need to prove to them that not only is it worth it, but that they'll be better people for doing so. If I can't, no one will buy in.

I constantly demonstrate that it is: by being prepared, by my work ethic, and by bringing other successful entrepreneurs into class, many of whom are former Babson students, who reinforce my philosophy.

You need to constantly be getting better.

Jack Welch, the former CEO of GE, said, "You should always upgrade your workforce every year by firing the bottom 10% and replacing them with better people." I completely agree.

Now, you're not going to do this in a vacuum; you're going to work with that bottom 10% to see if they can get (dramatically) better. But if they can't, or if you can find someone who can perform the work substantially better, you need to let go of the person who is not as good.

There are three reasons why.

First, if you don't, you're sending the message to the rest of your staff that less-than-stellar performances are okay.

Second, they're probably going to be happier working somewhere else where their performance will be in line with everyone else's.

And third, if you don't upgrade, you're going to fall behind your competition, who will.

MEMO TO EMPLOYEES

I believe in being totally honest with employees. There is no advantage in not being so.

Part of that honesty is explaining to them what is expected of them and how they will be evaluated.

Here are three points I think it is incumbent on you to explain to the people who work for you:

1. Remember that your efforts mean nothing to your employer unless they help him achieve his goals. You're not being paid for "trying." You're paid for your accomplishments.

2. Your company employs your labor if, and only if, it prefers it to anything else that it could do with its money—and that includes the labor of any other employee. You have no "right" to your job.

3. Your value to your employer depends solely on his ability to derive gains from your labor. (By "gains," I don't just mean monetary profits, but also everything else that matters to him and the organization.) If you have any doubts about this, see point #1.

THERE IS NO SUCH THING AS WORK–LIFE BALANCE

I know this will make some people cranky, but I believe it completely. Being the best at something requires hard work, a lot of time, and slavish devotion. If you're going to be putting in all that effort, everything else in your life is going be affected. There's simply no way around this fact, and that means there is no such thing as work–life balance.

When I say this, some people—invariably people who are passionately devoted to one thing such as building a company, becoming a world-class musician, or having the world's prettiest garden—agree with me.

As for the others, their responses tend to fall into three categories:

1. You're wrong.
2. Having my life be that far out of balance is not for me.
3. I will find a way around the problem.

Let's take them one at a time.

To people who tell me I'm wrong, I always respond: "You may be right. So, to show me the error of my ways, could you please give me the names of three people you know—or three people you have read or heard about—who are extremely high achievers and who didn't spend a disproportionate amount of their time working on what they're good at."

To this day, nobody has been able to come up with three names.

As for "it's not for me," that's more than fine. I understand (in theory, anyway) that people want balance in their life. If they can find it, and if it makes them happy, then I'm all for it—for them. They just need to recognize that it'll dramatically decrease their chances of becoming a high achiever in any one area. That is not a criticism, simply a matter of fact.

Finally, can you find a way around the problem? Well, you can certainly try. For example, let's say you have what I think are the mutually exclusive goals of being the world's best success in commerce—whatever you do for a living—and also being a world-class parent.

You know it is going to be hard, but you are committed, and so you decide you are only going to work from home. (This will give you the maximum amount of time you can spend with your kids.) You get up every day at four or five so you can get a bunch of work done before you have to get your children up for school. You pay complete attention as you make them breakfast and get them organized for their day. Once they're out the door, you work as hard as you can, knowing that your workday will end once the school day does. (There are sports practices to get to, extracurricular activities to attend, all that homework to get through.)

Then, maybe after you have made them dinner and tucked them into bed, you work a bit more, grab a few hours' sleep, and repeat the entire process again.

If you follow this course, have you achieved balance? Well, you have done it as well as it can be done, but you're still putting a limit on the upside of your career. You won't be able to manage people, and work-related travel will be difficult—or impossible. Because of these limitations—and others that are implicit in childrearing and the choices you've made—you're probably still going to be surpassed by people who can devote more time to their career.

There is absolutely nothing wrong with your choice if this is the life you want; just understand the limitations. (By the way, Jack Welch fully agrees with my analysis and goes one step further by calling it a "Work/Life Choice.")

BUT I FOUND THE SOLUTION! IF YOU WANT TO HAVE WORK–LIFE BALANCE, HAVE A SUPPORTIVE SPOUSE.

I think there is actually a way to achieve work–life balance: Have a spouse or partner who does all the things you don't.

I am very fortunate that my wife, Lois Green, did the vast majority of the childrearing and to this day runs 100% of our household. She's also extremely supportive of me and is an honest sounding board for my ideas.

Here's a quick example of how this played out.

Back when I was working for one of the major accounting firms, Deloitte Touche, I'd leave the house before the kids got up for school and didn't get back home until 8 P.M.

To make sure we had a semblance of a "normal" family life, Lois would feed the kids snacks in the late afternoon so that we could have a family dinner together the moment I walked in the door.

Obviously, the only way this kind of arrangement works is if both people are completely devoted to the roles they're going to play.

Does this mean women executives should pair up with a house-husband? Even though women—especially women who are mothers—are better, as a rule, than men at multitasking, my answer would be a resounding yes.

I've found the only way work–life balance truly works is by dividing everything up between two people.

There are limitations, no matter what option you choose. I was a good provider and I like to think I was a wonderful father, especially on family vacations, and I don't regret anything. However, I would be lying to you if I said I didn't feel a twinge of discomfort when my son, Jon Green, said to my grandchildren, "You're lucky that Grandpa is attending most of your games; he never went to all of mine."

IT'S NOT A MATTER OF PUTTING IN THE HOURS

To paraphrase former UCLA basketball coach John Wooden, who I mentioned before, you never want to confuse activity with accomplishment. The simplest example is: just because you show up at work every day doesn't mean you're getting anything done. In fact, thinking about the numbers of hours you work just confuses the issue. Time is not a factor; quality is. What does it take to get the job done right? Wooden believed that you had to follow a defined, planned-out routine that maximized efficiency until it became second nature to you. I do, too.

> It is not the time you put in; it's what you accomplish.
> Time served is only important when you are in jail.

Invariably that means a lot of preparation.

This is a lesson I try to get across to my students. Let me give you an example.

It happens early in the semester. I'll call on a student to discuss the case study that has been assigned, and they'll invariably say "I'm sorry, I didn't have time to prepare for it."

I'll say "I'm sorry you're not prepared. You can leave now."

The student is always shocked, and they usually say "But I still can get something out of the class if I stay and listen."

I tell them "I agree, but you'd have gotten so much more out of it if you were prepared; and equally important, coming to class unprepared is not how we do things. Please leave and return when you are prepared, and not before."

My approach may seem harsh—but I don't think so. To return to sports for a minute, it's exactly the way coaches prepare their teams. Their position is if you haven't been at practice, you won't play in the game. And all the great ones have every minute of practice fully scripted. They know exactly what they want to accomplish.

Here's a great example. I'm involved in the horse-racing business. One of my partners in a few horses I owned was Bobby Hurley. Bobby is now the head basketball coach of Arizona State University. Bobby was a first-team All-American at Duke in 1993, went to the Final Four three times, and led the Blue Devils in back-to-back national championships in 1991 and 1992, earning Final Four Most Outstanding Player honors in 1992.

Bobby told me the behind-the-scenes story of Duke's win in overtime during the NCAA "elite eight" tourney game in 1992.

Duke was losing by one point with less than a minute to play. Coach Mike Krzyzewski ("Coach K") called a time-out. He told the team it was going to win. He then outlined the next play. As time was expiring, Grant Hill threw a full-court pass to Christian Laettner, who turned around to make a jump shot that won the game.

Impossible as it seems, but Bobby told me they had practiced that situation many times so the players knew what to expect.

Coach K has a six-point plan for success. Here's how I interpret it: you don't wish for success; you prepare for it. Specifically, you:

1. Give attention to details and the big picture will take care of itself.
2. Adapt to changing conditions.
3. Play to win.
4. Have belief in your team members.
5. Are a good winner and a good loser.
6. Know it's okay to fail. It doesn't mean you're a failure, as long as you continue to strive for success and learn from your defeats.

ARE YOU MAKING THE MOST OF YOUR TIME?

Let me make one last point about the best use of your time.

Meetings are often just another example of confusing activity with accomplishment. Some managers have a monthly staff meeting, the weekly department meeting, and the daily "check-in" with immediate reports. These meetings sure fill up your calendar, but not much creativity—or anything else productive—comes out of them.

Why do so many managers have so many meetings?

First, for many managers, calling a meeting with a lot of attendees is a way they show off their power: "People literally have to come when I call." Second, there are some people—managers and employees alike—who can't get anything done without this kind of structure. Third, someone once told them that the key to leadership is to have a lot of meetings, so they have a lot of meetings.

My take on this is, if the manager has to have a lot of meetings, something is terribly wrong. On the other hand, if the executive, who has authority to make decisions, holds a meeting with a definite agenda that everyone is aware of, they can be very effective.

FOUR KEYS TO CREATING A PERSONAL COMPETITIVE EDGE

1. Be the first person in to work.
2. When the workday begins, be completely prepared to do your absolute best.
3. Be the last person to leave work.
4. Think about ways of improving your performance at your job when you are away from work.

PRIORITIZING

You're a hard-charging "type A" personality, so you have less of a problem than most concentrating on the right things. You'll naturally prioritize what needs to be done, concentrating on the most important things first.

But, can you help your people—especially the 80%—learn how to prioritize? Absolutely!

If you're doing something that isn't adding value,
don't do it.

You begin by asking simple questions such as "What are you working on, and why are you doing it?" Invariably, you'll find they are doing things that aren't adding value and/or could be done faster, cheaper, or better by someone else (either inside or outside your company).

You'll also discover that people will work on what they like doing to the detriment of all else. For example, salesmen will continue calling on the accounts that always give them an order and not go out and try to find new ones. They'll continually go after the proverbial low-hanging fruit.

To change that, point out that the only way the company is going to grow is by getting new accounts or selling more products or services to existing accounts. You may want to incentivize people to act the way you want. You might offer a bonus for every new account opened. (By the way, this same approach works for cutting costs.)

Avon Products has one of the most successful ways to incentivize salespeople. Every year, they invite their top salespeople and families to a sales conference. Awards are given out, with the highest performers receiving vacation trips for themselves and their families. Invariably, the salespeople who do not win trips one year are "incentivized" by their family to win a trip in the future.

I HAVE NO TIME FOR TIME MANAGEMENT

As we get into this subject of working hard, someone always asks me if there is a time-management system I use. I don't. I think the idea of using one is fraught with danger. Using such a system assumes that everything is predictable and that you're going to know how your day is going to go from the moment you walk into the office until you turn off the lights at night. But the world of an entrepreneur is never predictable.

This doesn't mean you respond immediately to every new thing that comes across your desk, or drop everything every time the phone rings. You always need to stay focused on the most important things you need to accomplish. You need to find a way to make that happen by delegating, automating functions, getting rid of parts of your job that sap your energy, and the like. You can't let the urgent overwhelm the important. Otherwise, you will just lurch from crisis to crisis.

However, I completely understand why people do. In a funny way, it's simply easier. Someone is yelling about a minor crisis they think needs to be resolved immediately and you deal with it. Once you have, you think you have accomplished something, but you really haven't. You're simply back to where you started before you knew the problem existed.

CASE STUDY: LEON HESS

 PROOF THIS WORKS

I am not about to canonize the man who created the oil giant Amerada Hess. However, he is the embodiment of what we are talking about.

Do you know what H-E-S-S stands for? Holidays and Every Saturday and Sunday. That "joke" came extremely close to describing the hours executives worked when he was CEO. Hess believed that he needed to outwork the competition, and if he had to put in those kinds of hours to do it, you did too.

The approach paid off. He followed the classic underdog playbook. Since he had limited resources when he started (all he had was a truck to deliver other people's fuel), he had to do things differently.

▸ Gas stations, at the time, were dirty, smelly places. Well then, Hess stations (and their bathrooms) would be immaculate. The employees would be dressed in white.

▸ Other stations had repair bays, which meant the customer did not always get prompt gas service. No repair bays at Hess meant attendants could always be at the pumps.

▸ Other gas stations didn't provide service. Hess employees always offered to check your oil and air pressure.

▸ If you always had the feeling that other stations were ripping you off with what they charged for gas, you wouldn't at Hess. The prices were always a couple of cents a gallon cheaper, partly because they did not accept credit cards.

All this makes sense, you say, but why the long hours at corporate headquarters? Well, to stay ahead of the competition, you needed to know what they were doing and that meant putting in a lot of time studying them. Then once you spotted an opportunity, you wanted to move quickly to capitalize on it. Working nights and weekends allowed Hess to be in constant contact with his team and allowed the company to make decisions faster.

There were rewards for putting in these kinds of hours:

1. Meals—breakfasts, lunches, and dinners—were free to employees.
2. Employees would get football tickets to the New York Jets (Hess owned the team).
3. If you or a family member became ill, you had access to the world's best doctors.
4. People who stayed with the company for a long time became extremely rich, thanks to stock options that became more valuable as the company grew.

The Hess approach worked for Mr. Hess, and the model has been used successfully for other entrepreneurs.

EXERCISE 6: HESS

1. What do you think of the Hess culture?

2. Would you be comfortable creating one like it?

3. Could you work there?

4. Could it work today?

5. Would it work after Mr. Hess retired?

6. What other inducements could Hess offer to attract good employees?

AS A BOSS, DO YOU HAVE TO BE AN SOB?

One last point: sometimes people worry that they're going to be perceived as being a son of a bitch if they demand the best out of everyone.

Is it a fair criticism? Maybe.

You certainly never want to be abusive or mean-spirited, but you do need to get the job done, and that can require some people doing more work—and more difficult work—than they want.

That, in turn, invariably will lead to some people calling you an SOB, which is really interesting. Once the job is done successfully and people have achieved more than they ever thought possible, they tend to look back at all those SOBs fondly and are grateful that they demanded their best.

How many football players who played under coach Vince Lombardi cursed him and the methods he used and the hours he made them put in? They constantly referred to him as an SOB—behind his back, of course.

After Lombardi's Green Bay Packers won multiple World Championships and many of the players like Jerry Kramer, Forrest Gregg, Paul Hornung, and Bart Starr became Hall of Famers, they praised Lombardi for his coaching methods and for getting the best out of them.

FOUR TAKEAWAYS FROM THIS CHAPTER

1. **There is no substitute for hard work.** None.

2. **If you are going to be successful . . .** that hard work is going to dominate your life. True "work–life balance" is a myth.

3. **But hard work without a game plan . . . is just hard work.** You need to know what you're trying to accomplish and develop the most efficient way of getting it. Otherwise, you could be wasting your time—or, worse, going in the wrong direction.

4. **You do need to be relentlessly focused on what is absolutely vital to accomplish.** You can't let the urgent overwhelm the important.

The Key Entrepreneurial Trait: Knowing How to Spot an Opportunity

How to spot an opportunity may be the key entrepreneur-ial trait, but you can't do it on an island. You can't simply wait for inspiration to strike and then suddenly realize "what the world truly needs is . . ." That is not how it works.

What do you do? You begin, in what you may think is an unusual place, by looking for opportunities to open your mind.

The longer you've been around, and the more successful you have been, the more difficult it'll be for you to accept new and/or different ideas, especially if those ideas don't correspond with the way you see the universe. When confronted with something that isn't within your usual frame of reference, you are likely to say, "This will never work."

You continue doing what you're doing because "if it isn't broken, why fix it?"

There are three problems with thinking this way, in addition to the obvious one—that you don't have a patent on all knowledge that exists now or ever will exist:

1. Even if you've mastered your corner of the universe, there are still millions of needs that require solving just around the corner.
2. Success can make you lazy. If what you're doing is working, there is little reason to think things could be performed better, faster, cheaper, or more efficiently.

3. Things change. To use an over-the-top example to make the point, it's terrific that you know all there is to know about VCRs, but if the world has moved on to digital recorders, that knowledge doesn't do you any good.

Here's the bigger point. The way you think—especially if you've been successful—may have locked you into a tight little corner. I'm sure that, for the longest time, back when the world was urged to (and did) "make it a Blockbuster night," the people at the video rental chain knew everything there was to know about renting movies. As a result, it never even occurred to them that someone could attack them (and their market) in a way they never thought of.

Netflix did, and the rest is history (as is Blockbuster).

Many people like to ask for input, but what they only want to hear is "Everything you are doing is perfect."

Don't be one of those people.

The next time you're tempted to dismiss a radically new idea out of hand, using the phrase "that will never work," think of Blockbuster. Then examine that "wacky" new idea in detail to see if it just might work.

HOW TO INCREASE YOUR CHANCES OF FINDING AN OPPORTUNITY

Notice what I didn't say in that headline. I didn't say, "By the time you are done reading this section, you are guaranteed to find an opportunity." Nope, there are no guarantees. Also, I didn't promise you that I'm going to provide a tried-and-true proven formula for spotting one.

First of all, the onus is on *you* to spot an opportunity that plays to your particular interests and strengths. Second, if it were all that simple and commonplace, everyone would do it. With all that said, here are some places you may want to look as you go searching for an opportunity.

First, start close to home. None of us is as unique as we think. If you—or your company—has a problem that needs solving, odds are that other companies and other people will too. Examples abound. Your little kids won't eat vegetables, so you create a mold that turns them into funny shapes, and suddenly you have a business shipping your tiny plastic molds worldwide. Your company spends a lot of time going from website to website trying to figure out which over-night shipper is cheaper to use for a particular package, so you create a software program that does the searching—and calculations—automatically. Suddenly, you have a new profit center.

Second, challenge conventional wisdom. No matter what you do for a living, there are certain rock-solid, unshakable beliefs in your industry. (These are ways business has always been done.) There may be no better example than Southwest Airlines.

Before Southwest Airlines, everyone knew that if you wanted to be a successful airline, you needed to fly to and from major airports using a hub-and-spoke model, and you had to provide the customer with an assigned seat. Everyone also knew that flying was serious business. No one went out of their way to entertain the customer or make the flying experience fun.

Southwest and its president Herb Kelleher ignored what everyone knew. Southwest flies point to point, there are no assigned seats, and the flight attendants try to make things fun for you with silly quizzes and offbeat safety demonstrations. The airline has thrived as a result.

If you think about approaching the market differently, you might come across an opportunity. Here are some ways to do things differently:

Upgrade. Take a basic product and make it special, either by adding value to it or marketing it as a status product. Luxury automobiles, coffee (Starbucks), and gourmet cookies are examples of what were once pedestrian products that have been given cachet. In each case, the underlying concept remains unchanged; it's just that the product's image has been improved. It's no longer merely a car, but a status symbol. Buying coffee becomes an experience, and cookies, once a simple, inexpensive treat, have become something worthy of an epicure. All that has really changed is the perception of these products—along with their price tag.

Perhaps the greatest example of this is water. It's hard to think of another product that has been upgraded in so many ways. (SoBe LifeWater, which comes in countless flavors; VitaminWater, the various flavored waters; etc.)

Downgrade. Take a product that has always been associated with status and reduce it to its underlying concept. Examples: Ryan Air in Europe eliminated all the frills that usually come with an airplane ticket. (Unfortunately, all the airlines are copying this model.) If you look on supermarket shelves, you now see everything from generic beer to house-brand cooking oil competing against Budweiser and Crisco.

Bundle. There are certain products or services that almost always go together. Instead of requiring people to pay for them separately, combine them. Most people have phones, Internet service, and TV subscriptions. And so the "triple play" packages from the phone and cable companies were born.

Unbundle. Just the flip side of what we discussed above. Ask yourself what products have been so gussied up that you can sell the individual components. Life insurance is a good example. It was common practice in the industry to combine the protection component with a savings element, which became the basic insurance policy. Term insurance, which eliminates the savings component and just provides protection, has become very popular.

Transport. If a product sells in one area, take it to another. Importer/exporters make their living this way. But you can go beyond just selling white wine from France in New Jersey. For example, Europe and California, for whatever reasons, tend to create new products and ideas ahead of the rest of the world. How about someone from Massachusetts taking a drive up and down the coast of California looking for new ideas in fast food, entertainment, whatever? Once you find what is working in Modesto, why not try it back home in Marblehead?

Mass-market. Take an idea that has been in one narrow area and see if it will work on a larger scale. This is what every company does when it takes a product "national."

Narrowcast. We borrow this term from television. When cable television was in its infancy, its broadcasters realized they all shouldn't try to reach mass audiences. For all their faults, the three networks did a fairly good job of that. The solution for cable operators was to narrowcast, or to gear shows on a given channel to a particular audience. Now you have channels that show nothing but sports or movies. There's even an all-weather station and a history channel.

Think big. Instead of carrying just one product, carry everything related to it. Think of the home improvement stores like Lowe's or Home Depot.

Think small. While huge stores, such as Lowe's, can offer more merchandise, they can't offer the depth of selection in each line that a true connoisseur demands. Also, they usually don't have a trained staff to offer advice. Your small local store can succeed by offering more in a small field like cabinets, rugs, and tile while providing advice and expert service.

CASE STUDY: R.C. BIGELOW

 *PROOF THIS WORKS*

Examining the history of the R.C. Bigelow Co., the large tea pur-veyor, reveals that for every opportunity you find, there is going to be at least one major problem to overcome.

At the start of World War II, Ruth Campbell Bigelow was a suc-cessful interior designer. As the war progressed, business slowed considerably, and she and her husband, David E. Bigelow, wanted to start a company that would be more stable. Ruth was a tea lover and had long been disappointed with the poor quality of tea in the United States. She had uncovered a recipe from the eighteenth cen-tury, for a blended tea that included orange rind and sweet spices. Ruth and David decided to develop this blended tea for sale.

Clearly an opportunity, right? Well, not an easy one to exploit. Five years in, sales were still hard to come by. Instead of looking at the negatives, the Bigelows looked for the positives. In examining what few sales they had, they realized a small gift shop in Connecti-cut was selling more of their tea than any other store. They visited the shop and saw that the owner had opened a canister of tea, allow-ing the customers to smell the aroma. Soon, a "whiffing jar" was in-cluded in every shipment to retailers. Sales soared.

The next move was into food services—that is, sales to restau-rants, cafeterias, hotels, and university dining halls. While a logical extension, it did not go well. By the mid-1970s, food service sales were less than 5% of total revenues. The problem was that Bigelow only offered the food services loose tea, which was very hard to han-dle, or individual tea bags packaged in tins. Having the servers pick out the bags one at a time was not sanitary, and the tea tended to dry out, since people didn't always remember to put the lid back on the canister. The solution? The company's introduction of a sealed, in-dividually foil-wrapped tea bag.

By the early 1980s, sales had stalled and costs were rising as two of the three suppliers of Bigelow's packaging closed (the remaining supplier raised its prices dramatically). So the company started selling the foil-wrapped tea bags within cardboard boxes that could easily be stacked on the supermarket shelf. And the company introduced "flavored tea," even though it was revolutionary! Could that work? You bet it did! The company now sells more than a billion tea bags a year.

EXERCISE 7: **BIGELOW TEA**

1. Are you surprised that Bigelow encountered a problem every time it tried to expand?

2. While the company has offered dessert spreads and coffee, the overwhelming majority of sales come from tea. Is that a good idea?

3. Should the company license its name?

4. Should the company be selling tea-flavored drinks, and, if so, how should it differentiate its product from competitors'?

WAYS TO JUICE YOUR THINKING

Knowing where to look is helpful, of course. Now, let's talk about six different ways you can increase your chances of finding a market opportunity.

1. Necessity. The cliché is right. Necessity really is the mother of invention. It's amazing how easy, when you're out of work and the bills are coming due you suddenly find opportunities. The same thing is true when you have a pressing personal need. You need a special diet and yet you can't find anything on the supermarket shelves that comes even remotely close to tasting good. You start creating meals for yourself and others like you, and all of a sudden you have a thriving company. Pepperidge Farms was started by a mother whose son needed bread made from natural sources.

2. Pay attention. That sage Lawrence Peter ("Yogi") Berra put it perfectly: "You can observe a lot of things just by watching." Simply by paying attention, if you were a woman of color back in the 1980s, you would have seen that cosmetic companies were ignoring the needs of black women, whose skin pigments were different from Caucasian women's. Along came Flori Roberts, who started a successful cosmetics company that catered to black women.

3. Bring back the suggestion box. Some of you may not even know what a suggestion box is, so let me explain. In its most basic and traditional form, it is a receptacle with an opening; picture a rectangular tissue box. The box is used for collecting slips of paper with input from customers and employees about what can be improved. It was a wonderful idea: Why not have the people, who do the work, suggest ways it can be done better? I like to take this idea one step further. To make sure I get the absolutely best suggestions, I offer an all-expense-paid vacation for two to the employee who comes up with the best idea. One year, the winner suggested a detailed social media strategy for our company—we had been lagging in this area—which resulted in bringing in a large number of clients.

> The harder you work, the "luckier" you get in spotting additional opportunities.

4. Think. I know I mentioned this before in a different context; but it's amazing how many opportunities you can find if you just give yourself some time to think. I go for long runs (without wearing headphones) and do marathons and always carry a pen and paper with me to capture all the ideas that inevitably spring to mind. You don't have to run long distances. Spend an extra five minutes in the shower; stare out the window for a while. Turn out the lights in your office and close your eyes and meditate after lunch. I don't care what you do, as long as you create some thinking time.

5. No Negative Nellies. If you want your staff to come up with as many good ideas as possible, you need to support them. You don't have to accept what they come up with—it's your company, after all—but you can't dismiss anything they suggest as "foolish" or "ill conceived." The moment you do, you'll never get a good idea again.

6. Study your competition. See what opportunities they're missing that you can take advantage of and figure out what they're doing right, so you can improve upon it.

PERCEPTION MATTERS

One of the things that people always say—whether you're talking about cutting costs or looking for a different way to do things—is "It can't be done." If you believe that, you're right. Your mindset will keep you from accomplishing anything new.

It really is an intriguing thing, because once somebody does what couldn't be done, the floodgates open and suddenly everyone is doing it.

Think back to Roger Bannister and the four-minute mile.

For decades, people said it was impossible for a human being to run a mile in less than four minutes. They pointed to physiological studies that said it couldn't be done. Everyone knew it couldn't happen.

And yet on May 6, 1954, in Oxford, Bannister turned in a time of 3 minutes, 59.4 seconds. Even more interesting than the fact that Bannister did it was what happened afterward. His record lasted just forty-six days; and within a year, fourteen other people had run the mile in under four minutes. Indeed, today running a sub-four-minute mile is commonplace. (The current world record is 3:43:13, a full sixteen seconds, or 5%, faster than Bannister's time.)

> It's amazing what new ideas you can come up with if you give yourself some time to think.
> Make sure you build that time into your schedule each day.

The point is that once someone destroys a myth, such as "It's impossible to run a four-minute mile," it becomes remarkably easy for new things to happen.

SOMETIMES IT HELPS NOT TO KNOW ANY BETTER

There is a natural tendency for people to look for opportunities in a field they know. That's the way most companies get started. You see an opportunity that your company is not taking advantage of, and when your boss tells you it is not worth pursuing, you decide to go off and do it on your own.

It doesn't have to be that way. In fact, there are certain advantages in entering a field you know little about. You don't know what the "rules" are, so you aren't handicapped by them.

That was the situation we encountered when we started Blue Buffalo. We didn't know much about pet food. But we did have expertise with distribution—thanks to the work done in developing

SoBe. But, more importantly, we had spotted a need. Bill Bishop, the president, had lost his dog Blue to cancer and was passionate about developing a very healthful pet food that had anticancer ingredients that could help pets live longer. Pet owners were also looking for more healthful food to give Spot and Kitty. So, we set out to hire the smartest people we could, people who knew the industry and wanted to help change it. We offered them more responsibility, money, stock ownership, and a chance to help create a new company. Bill was very innovative and created a culture that encouraged employees to make suggestions and recommendations. We were able to attract very good people who made our company a success, even though we didn't know much about the pet food business when we started.

CASE STUDY: THE TAYLOR MADE SALES AGENCY

 PROOF THIS WORKS

The horse-racing business is an interesting one. Unlike many other industries where the primary motivation is to make money, racehorse owners buy their horses for a number of reasons:

1. They love sports, but don't have the resources to buy a professional team.
2. They love the prestige of being an owner and going to the paddock to watch the horse saddled, talking to the jockey, and then going to the owner's box.
3. They enjoy bringing friends to the racetrack to watch their horses compete.
4. They find it thrilling to watch the horse they have selected and named run in the racing colors they have chosen.
5. They love the opportunity to be able to have their horse win. And they enjoy receiving the trophy and possibly being interviewed.

6. They can compete on equal footing with princes and billionaires, even though they may be just a part owner of a horse.
7. They are fascinated with legal gambling.
8. Of course, there is also the chance to make money through the winning of races, sale of their horses, and stud fees.

While the majority of racehorse owners are not profitable, many of the people who run businesses that service those owners are. Joe Lannon Taylor founded Taylor Made Sales Agency in Kentucky in 1976 and, along with his four sons, Duncan, Frank, Ben, and Mark, realized early on that they would need to constantly remain ahead of the pack to stay profitable.

Here are a few of their secrets of success:

1. First and foremost, they are excellent and knowledgeable horsemen.
2. Their farm, one of the country's leading thoroughbred consignors of horses, constantly experiments with adding new products and services. When the Japanese and Arabs became interested in the American horse-racing market, Taylor Made added employees who could speak these languages.
3. They were also one of the first to build state-of-the-art facilities to break yearlings and train young horses.
4. They equipped their barns with cameras so owners could always view their horses, no matter where they were.
5. They added staff who specialized in prepping horses so they would look their best at sales, and they used computers to keep track and become more knowledgeable about the habits of buyers (as a result, they notified their clients when Taylor Made was consigning horses that were related to horses their buyers had previously purchased).
6. They stressed customer service.
7. They treated customers and team members like their own family.
8. They gave their key employees a stake in their company so they felt like owners.

Taylor Made Sales has been in business for over forty years and continues to be North America's number one sales agency. To fully understand why Taylor Made is successful, their mission statement says it best.

Good people. Good Horses. Good Horsemen. We build personal and lasting relationships through honesty and transparency in all dealings; living and practicing the philosophy of the Agency's founder, Joseph Lannon Taylor, who inspired horsemen to always find a better way. We treat customers and team members like our own family; inspiring people to seek to be part of our culture which sees each person through an eternal perspective.

EXERCISE 8: **TAYLOR MADE**

1. Does adding all these services dilute the farm's focus?

2. Conversely, what else could it add to continue to stay in front of the competition?

3. Should the farm add more personal services to cater to its more successful clients? (Install a landing strip for private planes?)

4. Should the farm assign its top clients to a "personal representative and adviser," someone who would be available 24/7 to assist them?

5. Does diversification make sense? Offering stallions for breeding? Why? Why not?

6. If they do go into the breeding business, how do they, with a limited budget, obtain the sires to do the breeding?

7. Should they start their own auction company to buy and sell horses?

8. At what stage should the four sons begin thinking about succession planning?

FOUR TAKEAWAYS FROM THIS CHAPTER

1. **Be methodical about every part of your business, including how you go about spotting an opportunity.** Don't leave it—or anything else—to chance.

2. **Devote a specific amount of time each day—every day—looking for opportunities.**

3. **As you look for opportunities, start close to home.** If you have a problem that needs solving, odds are others will too.

4. **Think differently.** Examine the way business has always been done in the industry you want to participate in, and look for ways to challenge conventional wisdom.

Successful Entrepreneurs Are Not Risk-Takers; They Are Calculated *Risk-Takers*

Here's a question most of my students get wrong, and you likely will too. (Don't feel bad; just about everyone answers it incorrectly.)

Ready? What is the number one characteristic of an entrepreneur? (Hint: If you read Principle 5 carefully, you know.)

The vast majority of my students—and everyone else I ask— usually say, "They're risk-takers." If I'm feeling generous, I'll reward my students with partial credit for this answer, but I probably shouldn't.

The number one characteristic of successful entrepreneurs is that they are *Calculated* Risk-Takers. The difference between risk-takers and calculated risk-takers is the difference between failure and success.

Risk-takers bet it all on one roll of the dice. If they fail, they fail spectacularly—and in such a way that they *don't* live to fight another day. They literally go out in a blaze of attempted glory.

This is not what the best entrepreneurs do. They figure out a way to reduce risk with every step they take. They follow the Act. Learn. Build. Repeat. model that we talked about in Principle 4 and they take small steps toward their goals. Before they take those small steps, they figure out a way to minimize their modest investment even further. They ask, "How can I take this step more cheaply (and/or by using someone else's money); how can I do it faster (so I don't have to invest as much time), and how can I do it better than I had initially planned?"

Indeed, the process of minimizing risks begins long before you take this first step:

▸ What are others doing wrong?
▸ What are others doing right?

Let's start at the beginning. Before you make any move to create a new product or service, you want to study not only the specific area where you think you're going to concentrate, but also the industry as a whole, in order to be able to select a niche where you can excel. (You can see why this principle—which deals with minimizing risks—follows the last one, How to Spot an Opportunity.)

No, you will never know what's truly going on in a market before you enter it. And no, you don't want to do a lot of homework, because you don't want your potential opportunity to pass you by while you are doing research. But before you invest your time and money, you do want to gain a thorough understanding—either by yourself or by creating a team of people who have knowledge of the industry—of what the competition is doing.

Almost always, when I say this, people instantly jump to what the competition is doing wrong and what opportunities they're missing. And it is, indeed, an extremely important thing to do. You want to find places that they may have overlooked, or could be underserving. The list in the last chapter—where we talked about the importance of upgrading, downgrading, bundling, etc.—could help you a lot here.

What you want to do is find ways you are different.

MINIMIZING RISKS 101

If you're going into business with other people, the Act. Learn. Build. Repeat. model we talked about in Principle 4 is a great way to minimize the risks that come with starting a new company.

But even before you take your first steps toward creating anything new, there are things you can do administratively to reduce your risks even further. For some of you, the following advice is going to seem basic, but you would be amazed by how many people don't take one or more of these following four steps:

1. Form a business organization/entity that provides tax and business flexibility and protects your assets. I usually recommend a Limited Liability Corporation (LLC) so creditors cannot go after your personal assets should your venture fail.

2. Have liability insurance.

3. If you have partners, create an operating agreement that covers what happens to the business if one of you dies, gets divorced, becomes seriously ill, or leaves the business.

4. Create a buy/sell agreement. Agree on criteria for the valuation of the company. I recommend that the agreement reflect that the parties will agree on a valuation expert to establish the valuation, and that that decision is binding.

These four simple steps go a long way toward minimizing risks.

Important Note: Draw up this arrangement as the venture is just getting under way. It'll be easier to get everyone in agreement, since no one will know who might be affected in the future.

For example, you run a small hardware store and see that Home Depot and Lowe's are moving into your neighborhood. Instead of saying, "We're doomed," really study their stores. If you do, you'll see that their very size can be used against them. Sure, they carry just about everything, but it's extremely difficult to find any one specific item within their acres of selling space and their service—to be kind—is spotty. If you have a helpful staff and carry most things that people need to fix up and enjoy their homes, you should continue to do very well.

And don't forget to look at what the competition is doing right: that's another way of minimizing risk. There may be a way to build off what they have already proven to work. This is one of our great strengths at Blue Buffalo pet food company. We now have more than six hundred different product offerings. Most of the ideas stem from our CEO, Bill Bishop, who was also the marketing man behind SoBe beverages. Bill is always keeping his eye on the competition. While I've never stopped to count, my guess is that a large number of the ideas for our new products came from an improvement of a competitor's product.

For example, Blue Buffalo saw that one of the smaller pet-care companies was selling a new kind of kitty litter, one made from wood chips. We started looking into the concept of using wood, and eventually that led us to begin experimenting with crushed walnut shells, which proved to be an excellent deodorizer. Our walnut-based kitty litter is a solid seller for us.

> Minimizing risks should be an integral part of your company's strategy. I can't begin to tell you the number of companies that get lax about this as they grow, always to their detriment.

Often people resist borrowing (and then improving) ideas that someone else had first. This is just silly. If your intent is to reduce the chances of failing, why wouldn't you want to borrow something that has already proven to be successful and improve upon it, taking advantage of your strengths? In Blue Buffalo's case, once we improve an existing idea, we can plug the product into our distribution networks. Stores are always looking for new products. Blue Buffalo has grown in sales and shelf space by constantly adding new products our customers want to buy.

> You can't assume you know everything. If you think you do, it will cripple your organization.

You shouldn't care about where the idea was invented if it helps solve your customers' needs. The idea is to always deliver new products and services as cheaply and simply as possible, with little risk, while providing value that the customer will appreciate.

MORE THAN MONEY IS AT RISK

When we talk about minimizing risks, people instantly think we are talking about reducing the risk of the money they are investing. While this is important, there are six other risks that you should also consider when you're creating something new:

1. Time. Time is a finite resource, so you want to guard your time as much as you guard your money. Just as you have a dollar figure that would be "acceptable" to lose if the venture doesn't work out, you want to have a time limit as well. You need to say, "I'm willing to give this idea up to six months to see if it'll work. After that, I'm going to try something else."

2. Missed Opportunities. If you're working to start venture X, you can't be working on venture Y at exactly the same moment—though Y may be a far better idea. In business schools, this concept is referred to as "opportunity cost"—the cost of not pursuing other things. You want to be mindful of what you're choosing not to do. You also want to recognize another form of opportunity cost: the price to be paid for not acting right away. Someone else might implement your idea. Then there is the price to be paid for inaction; you might spend the rest of your life in a job you hate because you missed a great opportunity.

3. Professional Reputation. We all have one, although when you're first starting out, it may be extremely slight. As I've said, there's nothing wrong with failing if the idea you tried was worthy, you were sufficiently committed to it, and you learned from the experience. If you did those three things, then failure isn't fatal. But, if you're seen as someone who doesn't anticipate obvious problems, or who can't conserve resources and use them properly, that failure can seriously hurt you in the future. You may find it far harder to raise money or even to get another opportunity. Damage to your professional reputation can be a huge loss.

4. Personal Reputation. You don't want your new venture to be an embarrassment, which could affect your self-esteem or fail to represent who you truly are. This kind of loss is similar to the loss of a professional reputation, but literally it hits much closer to home. Losing your standing with those near and dear to you, or within your religious community or civic group, can be devastating. Unintelligent or frequent avoidable failures are embarrassing and carry psychosocial consequences. Moreover, as we discussed, one of the primary sources of funding for your venture is likely to come from your family and friends. You certainly don't want to waste their money (and good graces), especially if the money is coming from your in-laws. In addition, the time you'll be spending on the new venture will keep you away from people you care about, so you want to choose extremely carefully, whatever you plan to do, to make the loss of spending time with them worthwhile. This brings us to the next point.

5. Relationships. Starting anything new is stressful—emotionally and financially. It's easy for that stress to spill over into your relationships with your spouse and kids.

6. Your Health and Sanity. I wish I were exaggerating, but I'm not. If you're not careful, the stress of starting a new business can jeopardize both.

Finally, we get to the question of money. Obviously, you never want to waste it. That's why you do research before you begin, to make sure that there's an opportunity. This is why you take small steps—to ensure that you don't get too far off course—once you're under way.

Again, you only invest the amount of money you and your other investors can afford to lose. But—and this is a huge but—you need to have a Plan B to raise more capital if the situations warrant it.

There are three commonplace scenarios that could cause you to need more money:

1. The venture is taking longer than you thought. That's why—as mentioned before—I recommend that you budget as if you'll have no income in the first year and assume that everything will end up costing 30% more than your highest estimate. You want to have a substantial safety net.

2. You are close. You've hit on the right path. All the signs are positive, but you need more cash to break through.

3. Things are going better than you could have dreamed and people are asking for additional products and larger orders than you anticipated. You never want to have to say, "I'd love to do it, but I just don't have the working capital."

CASE STUDY: PIZZA

The more you look at the stats, the more you are convinced you're on to something.

- ▶ Americans eat more than 350 slices of pizza per second.
- ▶ Ninety-three percent of Americans eat *at least* one pizza pie a month.
- ▶ Pizza is a $30 billion-a-year industry.
- ▶ More people start pizzerias than any other restaurant.

▸ Pizza accounts for more than 10% of all food service sales.

You're convinced. You're going to enter the pizza business. What can you do to minimize your risks?

EXERCISE 9: **PIZZA**

1. Is location, location, location the most important element in deciding to open your restaurant?

2. Are you, in fact, going to do retail? Why and why not?

3. Are you going to have seating, or just take-out service?

4. If you decide not to go retail, how're you going to handle distribution? Who will you be selling to?

5. How're you going to position your offering: upscale (gourmet), or downscale (99 cents a slice)? In other words, as you think about it, is pizza a commodity, or an eating experience?

6. Are you planning to sell more than one kind of pizza?

7. Are you going to offer Italian food as well? Why or why not? If yes, how are you going to offer it: in-store only, takeout only, or in store *and* takeout?

8. Are you going to buy a franchise and sell franchise brand-name pizza?

9. How important are the people who work for you, and why?

10. Are you going to have delivery service?

11. What are you going to do to enhance the experience of the buyer?

This is a great exercise, because by this point you should be "thinking differently" than you were before you started reading. Do you realize what has changed?

The more differently you think, the more habit forming it becomes, increasing your chances to be successful.

ARE YOU SURE YOU WANT TO DO THAT?

One way to minimize mistakes is by not making them in the first place. A good way to try to do this is to have your employees and advisers give you honest feedback on the ideas you'd like to implement.

We all say we want this, but most of us don't. As we said before, we want people to tell us that our latest idea, just like all of our ideas, is brilliant. Obviously, that isn't always going to be the case.

Encourage people to speak up when they think you're on the wrong track and reward them when they raise reasonable concerns and objections. You don't have to take their advice, but it would be a good idea for you to think about their objections. People rarely tell the boss he is all wet without seriously thinking about it first.

FOUR TAKEAWAYS FROM THIS CHAPTER

1. **Be risk averse.** Perhaps the biggest misconception about entrepreneurs is that they're risk-takers. They are not. They're *calculated* risk-takers.

2. **Don't gamble with your future.** Risk-takers are *not* successful, as a rule. The reason for that is simple: they leave too much to chance.

3. **Remember: money is the fuel that keeps your organization running.** Make sure you have more than enough when you begin, and then manage what you have carefully.

4. **Receive honest feedback, minimize risks.** If you own a business, I strongly recommend that you create an advisory board (something we are going to talk about in Principle 9) and empower all employees to tell you when you're about to do something wrong or when they have a better idea (reward them for their candor).

You—Yes, You—
MUST Have an Advisory Board

Does the following reaction sound familiar?

I know I should have an advisory board. However, after putting in ninety hours a week, for Lord knows how long, and finally turning my company into a success, you want me to bring in people who don't know my business to give me their thoughts? You want me to pay them for their opinions when they have no real skin in the game, then seriously contemplate what they have to say knowing:

- They never walked a mile in my shoes.
- Once they walk out of my conference room, they may not spend a minute thinking about my business until just before the next meeting.

Have an advisory board? No, thank you.

A lot of entrepreneurs feel this way. Are they wrong? If you are picturing a board like that, advisers who are dilettantes or retired businesspeople with nothing better to do than offer platitudes to you, then you're probably not wrong.

But why would you ever have a board made up of people like that?

Let's take a step back and discuss why you would want an advisory board in the first place, before we go into detail to explain why it is a good idea.

WHY YOU NEED A BOARD

Entrepreneurs are reluctant to change, and that is especially true if they've been successful. When things are finally going well, the natural tendency is to look around and say, "Everything is great; there is no reason to alter anything. If it ain't broke, don't fix it."

What's the problem with that? A lot.

First, things are going to change, whether you like it or not. New competitors will enter your industry; the economy is going to tank or take off; your most important customer may wake up one morning and decide she would prefer to do business with someone else. Very few things are within your total control.

Second, you get into a rut when things are going well or worse, you may be feeling tired. Putting in ninety-hour weeks is exhausting, and "only" working sixty—or maybe even fifty, now when things are going well—is so much more pleasant. Once you make the decision to cut back, things begin to slip or fall through the cracks, and new projects start to take longer to implement.

The third point is directly related to the second. New ideas become harder to come by when you're not putting in the time to truly study what the competition is doing and what customers really want.

The upshot: You keep doing things your old way, and your business begins to slip. Or, as you grow, you begin to encounter problems you've never faced before, and you realize it would be beneficial if you could discuss these challenges with others who have successfully solved them.

These are the starting points as to why you need a board of advisers. They can keep you focused on the things that matter.

Now, let's walk through these extremely specific places where they can help you, along with details of the composition and workings of the board.

HOW ARE YOU REALLY DOING?

You always want honest feedback. Sure, most of your ideas are good ones, given your track record, but everyone has a huge clunker every once in a while, and it sure would be nice to prevent that from happening if you could. You expect your staff to tell you when your ideas are not the best.

1. But this may not always happen.
2. Given the fact that your staff works for you, you may tend to discount their opinions. As a result, you run the risk of not getting solid feedback.

That's where a good board of advisers can come in handy.

I want to be clear about this. You want your board of advisers' feedback and ideas, but you have the final call.

You always want to surround yourself with people who have alternative points of view.

The way you handle your board's feedback should be identical to how you handle it elsewhere in your life. If you think it makes sense, you take the suggestions. If they don't, you don't. The obvious advantage is, if you have a good advisory board, you're going to get lots of suggestions and ideas that you haven't thought of and different points of view and alternative ways to solve problems you're facing.

CASE STUDY: WEST CONSTRUCTION

If ever there was a situation where a board of advisers could have helped, this is it. Jerry West, twenty-eight, is about to graduate (with high honors) from Babson's MBA program, and he has two solid job offers. One is from a multinational company based in

Houston, with a starting salary of $80,000 a year. The other comes from a relatively small, but rapidly growing, specialty food company in San Francisco. They will start him at $70,000, saying, "You can advance as far and as fast as your talents allow." Jerry's bride of six months says she'll let him decide where they're going to live. She is a fledgling, talented decorator (a big-city girl from the West Coast), so she would prefer San Francisco.

Following graduation, the couple heads out to Utah to visit Jerry's folks. His father owns a $10 million construction company in rural Utah, where Jerry happily worked every summer since he was fourteen. There have been occasional comments made by his parents (pointing to the construction offices) that "someday all this will be yours, Jerry," but nothing more than that has ever been said.

His dad is sixty and in excellent health. Jerry's two siblings have shown no interest in taking over the business; one plays in a rock band and the other is a stay-at-home parent. The fact that his dad hasn't mentioned anything about Jerry taking over led Jerry to believe they were not counting on him. (That's why he decided to go to business school in the first place.)

This visit changes everything. His parents tell him that his uncle, the second in command of the firm, is retiring and add, "The timing has worked out perfectly for you to join the company and begin preparing to take over." There is talk about his father staying on "until you're ready to take the reins," but no time frame is given and it's clear that his father expects to make the turnover decision unilaterally. While the offers Jerry received from the two other firms were certainly "flattering," his dad said, "You can't expect to start here at those kinds of salaries. Maybe we can go as high as $60,000."

Complicating the picture, Jerry's parents want to be "fair," so for "the time being" his father will own 50% and his mother will own 20% of the company, and the three children will split the remaining shares. While Jerry truly likes the construction business, and sees the possibilities of what it can become, his wife hates the idea of living in "Middle-of-Nowhere, Utah."

EXERCISE 10: WEST CONSTRUCTION

1. Should Jerry join the business?

2. What recommendations could an independent board of advisers have made as to:
   a. Jerry's father years ago
   b. Jerry years ago
   c. Jerry now, to attract him to the firm
   d. Changing the ownership structure
   e. A reporting structure
   f. What would be palatable to Jerry and his father
   g. The entire West family to help them deal with the emotional component of all this

3. What would be a "win-win" solution for Jerry, his dad, his wife and her career, and the family business?

NETWORKING

In addition to being smart, creative problem solvers, the people on your board should also be accomplished. They should have achieved some success; met a lot of smart, talented, and successful people along the way; and be in a position to introduce you to them.

Suppose you are looking for additional financing, and banks are charging too much interest and making unreasonable demands for collateral. When you bring your board of advisers up to date on this challenge, it would be extremely helpful if one of them says, "You know, I was having lunch the other day with old Fred. You guys remember Fred, right? He made a ton of money when Old Fred Corp went public. He told me he would like to start backing emerging growth companies like this one. The $10 million we need is about the size of an investment he's hoping to make. If it's okay with you, [Ms. Entrepreneur/CEO], I'll give him a call and introduce you two."

Or perhaps you're thinking of expanding internationally and

you really aren't sure how to do it. Again, hopefully someone on your board has had to handle the exact same problem. Equally important, they'll be willing to share their "networking list" with you to introduce you to experts you can call on as you head overseas.

MENTORING

We all need help from time to time. For an entrepreneur, one of the biggest challenges is usually succession planning, and it usually falls to the bottom of the entrepreneur's "to-do" list. It's not surprising for an entrepreneur to wake up one day at the age of sixty, sixty-five, or seventy to find that they really don't have a succession plan.

Your board can be a huge help here, simply by constantly raising the topic at meetings and reminding you it needs to be done. Eventually, if for no other reason than you want them to stop bugging you, you'll address the issue.

But perhaps the biggest role an advisory board plays is being someone the CEO can talk to. It really is lonely at the top; having someone to bounce ideas off of, or simply having someone to discuss challenges with, can be invaluable.

Mentoring your staff, and even your family, is another place your board can help. Some executives get flustered if the boss tries to give them feedback. They concentrate so much on the fact that the person who signs their paycheck is offering suggestions and/or criticism that they can't fully concentrate on the advice itself. Having a member of your board—instead of you—coach them can help a great deal.

The other thing they can do is to serve as a mentor for members of your family. This can be true whether or not family members are part of your business. Obviously if they are, there can be conflicts that have little or nothing to do with the business itself. It can be difficult working for/with your spouse, brother, sister, or parent. Having someone from the outside who can moderate/referee/coach can help.

Even if your kids aren't in the business, members of your advisory board can serve as mentors to them. As every parent has learned the hard way, children don't always listen to their parents. They may pay attention to an accomplished member of your advisory board.

THE COMPOSITION OF YOUR BOARD

Having laid out the foundation, let's spend some time discussing how all this can work. The most basic question first: Who should be on your board?

Let me begin my answer in the negative: Don't include people who are your company's accountants, lawyers, senior executives, or bankers, because they all have a vested interest in pleasing you. They are beholden to you for work—and income. You can always choose another accountant (or accounting firm), lawyer, or banker—and they know that. They have a vested interest in making you happy and, as such, have a potential conflict of interest.

Yes, you want your business to have an accountant, lawyer, and banker, but they shouldn't be on your board. They're already giving you advice.

If not these people then, who? I'll answer that question in a moment. First, let me flag an important point that might make having a board of advisers even more palatable to you.

They serve at your pleasure

Unlike the board of directors at a publicly held company, which is answerable to the shareholders, an advisory board is answerable only to you. This means you can fire them any time you want—and you should if it's clear that they aren't adding value.

There's a difference between their offering solid ideas you don't want to accept and not adding value. But if it becomes clear, after a reasonable period of time, that all they're doing is taking up space, then you should fire them.

So what types of people are going to add value? I want board members who:

▸ Are honest
▸ Are independent problem solvers, reflecting the kind of values I have
▸ Can add industry knowledge
▸ Have the networking possibilities that we mentioned
▸ May be of financial assistance (personally, or through referrals)
▸ Have a passion to be on the board

PROCEDURES

Let's talk about how this plays out in practice. You can set up your board any way you want, but let me share what works for me.

I like our boards to meet quarterly. More frequently, and we end up discussing the day-to-day minutiae; less frequently, and small problems can become large ones before we can get around to dealing with them.

SHOULD FAMILY MEMBERS BE ON THE BOARD?

I know some people disagree, but I think it's important your spouse and children be part of the advisory board, even if they aren't part of the company itself. Since the business is so important to you, and indirectly to them, they should be involved.

I insist that they follow the rules when they attend meetings. Board meetings are not the place to discuss family issues and conflicts. They're attending to gain a better understanding of the business and to ask questions only about the business.

How many people should be on your board? I find somewhere between six and ten works well. More than that, and it can get unwieldy; fewer than that, and you don't have enough differing opinions.

Speaking of diversity, I think it's extremely important. Some people think they should have board members who offset their weaknesses. If they're a marketing guy, then they concentrate on having people on their board in finance and technology. I think that's exactly the wrong way to go.

> When it comes to creating a board of advisers, you're building a team. All the team-building rules apply.

So, what am I looking for (in addition to smart, creative problem solvers) when I pick my board? I want a mix of calculated risk-takers as well as conservative people to help ground us. Do they have to have extensive business experience? Well, it's helpful but not always necessary. For example, in earlier years, Rabbi Jack Rosoff was one of my advisers because of his unique sensitivity and conflict-management skills, which he used daily as a clergyman.

It could be helpful if you knew your business was going to go in a new direction—you are going to buy a company in a different market segment or you'll be expanding internationally—if your board members have expertise in those areas. Is it absolutely required? No. You'll be amazed by how many people your board members know.

They don't have to be experts on what you do, but you do want differing perspectives. Not only is it important to generate more and better ideas, it also sends a positive message to your staff. If you have young people and women on your board, it reinforces to the young people and women in your company that they are important.

Let's discuss what happens when the board actually gets together.

WHY WOULD THEY SERVE?

Given that they're accomplished individuals, there are going to be numerous demands on the time of the people you'd like to serve on your board. So, you have to come up with a good reason—and perhaps more than one—why they should.

Not surprisingly, it all ties to the Maslow hierarchy of needs:

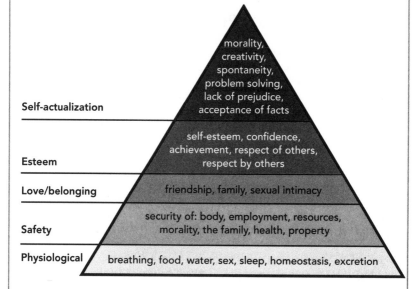

Self-actualization — morality, creativity, spontaneity, problem solving, lack of prejudice, acceptance of facts

Esteem — self-esteem, confidence, achievement, respect of others, respect by others

Love/belonging — friendship, family, sexual intimacy

Safety — security of: body, employment, resources, morality, the family, health, property

Physiological — breathing, food, water, sex, sleep, homeostasis, excretion

Let's start at the bottom of the triangle. Money—as in their compensation—is a factor, but not the deciding factor. For my board meetings, I pay people $200 an hour and all their expenses. In addition, advisory board members are often given other benefits such as stock options, or the ability to buy shares at a discount. Even though money isn't the main reason someone will serve, no one has ever turned down the check.

There are factors farther up the Maslow hierarchy that come into play.

You're appealing to their ego; it's flattering to serve on someone's board. Also, having the chance to get in on the ground floor of something, and help shape a company's future, gives them bragging rights for their contributions.

Two last points.

Never waste their time. Always show your gratitude.

HOW THE MEETINGS SHOULD WORK

I recommend using the following outline so you maximize the benefit of an executive board.

About a month before the meeting, board members get a package that contains the minutes of the last meeting, along with a note asking what topics they want to discuss this time. If there is nothing specific they want to discuss, I create an agenda. If they have specific concerns, I will make sure they are addressed. I also ask what information they want to see ahead of time (financials, projections, strategies, etc.) so they have what they need to make solid contributions at the meeting.

They get the agenda about ten days before the meeting so they have time to prepare. The meeting—running a few hours to all day, depending on what needs to be discussed—is always divided into three parts.

1. Business. We discuss their issues plus what I want their advice on.

2. Mentoring. Who needs help, both inside and outside of the company? (We'll set up a schedule where the board members can work with these people.)

3. Social. There's always a dinner the night before or after the meeting. Once a year we hold the meetings off-site at a resort or some other nice venue, and the advisory board members are encouraged to bring their spouses. An advisory board is a team, and the social aspect is a good way to try to forge close bonds among the members.

FOUR TAKEAWAYS FROM THIS CHAPTER

There are numerous advantages to having a board of advisers. If you only remember these four, you'll do just fine.

1. **Honest Feedback.** It's nice to think your employees will tell you the truth, the whole truth, and nothing but the truth when you ask for their opinions. This isn't always the case with people who receive their paycheck from you. Your board of advisers doesn't have these conflicts. Yes, you are paying them, but it isn't enough to get them to sugarcoat their opinions.

2. **Networking.** Ideally, your advisers will know people who can help your business grow (a factor you should be looking for when looking for board members).

3. **Opinions and Problem Solving.** You always want to consider different points of view and different ways of solving problems. Your advisers should be a big help here. (If they're not giving you new perspectives, they shouldn't be on your board.)

4. **Mentoring.** You may need to improve in certain areas; your board could help you and the people who work with you.

Research the Market;
Narrow the Options; Act!

Henry Ford once said, "If you asked people who have a horse and buggy what they want, they will probably say a faster horse."

It is a good point. People are not always good at envisioning the kind of new products they need. It is up to you to create alternatives for them.

The questions are always the same, whether you're someone barely out of your teens starting your first venture, or a serial entrepreneur:

1. How do you know you truly have a good idea?
2. How do you know that the idea is absolutely the best one to pursue?

Surprisingly, the path you take to find out the answers is the same in either case.

Invariably, if you're inside—or used to be part of—a big company, your first inclination is to study the problem to death to make sure you have the best idea possible. You'll survey the marketplace; read every analyst report ever written; visit with hundreds of potential customers. Only then do you come up with prototypes or mockups that you subject to endless market research and focus groups.

But the time you're done with all that, someone else may have taken advantage of the customer need you've spotted, or the market has moved on.

No, the best way to do research—as we talked about before—is to go into the marketplace and ask someone to buy what you have.

I want to expand on that point for a second. The key is: Will they buy what you're offering? If you ask if they like the product or service you're thinking of offering, they'll probably say, "Yes," if for no other reason than to be polite. They know you've worked hard to come up with this idea, and they don't want to hurt your feelings.

> There's a huge problem with market research in general and focus groups in particular. People tell you what they think you want to hear instead of the truth.

That's why you want to know if they're actually willing to pay for your potential offering. If, as the cliché goes, they're willing to put their money where their mouth is, you're probably on to something. The moral here: It's wonderful that people say nice things about your product, but don't take those kind words too seriously until they pull out their checkbook.

RESEARCH CAN BE A CRUTCH

When I see someone being overly dependent on doing research before going ahead with trying to sell a product or service, I think to myself, "This person is not a calculated risk-taker." She can't figure out if what she has is worth pursuing, and she's too timid to take the idea to the market.

You can't go anywhere if your boat is tied to the dock.

THE RESEARCH YOU SHOULD DO

So, does this mean you do absolutely no research? No. You only do the minimum necessary. That being said, as we alluded to earlier, one area you don't want to skimp on is what your competition is doing. For one thing, odds are that they've probably invested in a lot of expensive and comprehensive research—the bigger the firm, the more research they've probably done—and you can then piggyback on their work. For another, your next opportunity could come from just "improving" what they've introduced. It's remarkable the number of additional opportunities you'll be able to think of once you see the new product/service they have unveiled. You can improve on what they have and prosper. It really makes sense to see what the competition is doing, in order to determine if you can improve on it.

GENERATING THE IDEAS

There are some people who believe that when it comes to researching the market, you want to be remarkably focused from the beginning. You should try to come up with one big idea almost immediately and then refine it—correcting flaws, adding and eliminating features, etc. They will tell you this is the most efficient approach, one that allows you to move the fastest.

I disagree. You want to get as many ideas as you can—and have those ideas, if possible, come from many different sources. If you surround yourself with people who are just like you—your age, background, and experience—you will, not surprisingly, get similar ideas. Get people of different ages, backgrounds, and experiences in the room; explain the challenge ("We need to expand"); and let the ideas fly.

Ideas don't need to be targeted toward solving a specific problem. You can hold idea-generating sessions—and there are countless books and people who can help you do that—where the goal is "just" to come up with as many ideas as possible.

Let me stress this: You need to take the process seriously. If people suggest good ideas and those ideas are feasible, you need to give them a try. The worst thing you can do is what a major corporation did. They sent their middle and senior managers on a corporate retreat for a couple of days. The idea was to generate new ideas, and working as a team, they came up with dozens. They then narrowed the list down to a handful they thought would have the most impact on the company. They went back to work and presented their best. Unfortunately, top management told them, "They will never work." Not one of those ideas was even tried.

Do you want to guess whether those people volunteered any ideas again?

THINGS CHANGE

The fascinating thing about researching the market the way we are talking about is that while the approach you take doesn't change, you do, and the market does as well. New players are entering the field all the time; market conditions shift; your competitors do new things.

But the biggest thing that probably changes is you.

You get older, more experienced. You get exposed to more, and so you have a more refined frame of reference. The more you look at something, the more knowledgeable you become.

That's why, if you are relatively new in business, drawing on advisers can be a very good thing. They will have the experience you lack.

HOW DO YOU BEGIN TO NARROW DOWN THE OPTIONS?

Once you come up with a list of promising ideas, you need to narrow down the list, and how you do it depends on where you are in your company's evolution and your own career.

If you're just starting out and money is extremely tight, you need to concentrate on the idea that has the ability to start generating revenues quickly. If it's going to take $100 million to get under way and there's absolutely no way you can raise that kind of money, it doesn't make any sense to pursue a market that may be worth billions. You'll simply run out of funding before you get anywhere near the finish line. (As we talked about before, you never want to run out of money on your first venture. If you do, it'll be extremely difficult to persuade anyone to fund you for a second attempt.)

As your company gets a bit more established—say you're researching your second venture—you have a bit more flexibility when it comes to what you want to pursue. For example, you may have come up with two truly wonderful ideas. While one has the potential to have twice the sales of the other, you're absolutely passionate about the smaller of the two. In this case, you may decide to pursue your passion. Pick the best idea, based on where you and your company are in your evolution, and don't look back.

SLOW HORSES AND BAD IDEAS

There are a number of reasons why the horse-racing business is fascinating. Here's one of my favorites.

Most horses are sold at yearling sales (when the horses are one year old). The buyer can inspect the horse and watch it walk to see how physically correct its stride is. This is a good indication of how well the horse will run and how physically sound it will stay. They will also look at its pedigree, but not much else. Other horses are sold at two-year-old sales (when the horses are two), and there the buyer can watch the horse walk and work in "short workouts," as they run over small distances, which is somewhat helpful. But since the actual races the horses will run in are longer distances, you have to make an educated guess on how the horse will perform when it counts.

Therefore, it's not uncommon after a buyer has spent hundreds of thousands of dollars buying a potential racehorse to discover that it simply can't run very fast for a longer distance in actual races. This is clear when the horse finishes substantially out of the money after a number of races. Many owners refuse to admit they've made a mistake. Instead, they will blame the circumstances—"It was a slow track" or an external factor; "He has gotten a lousy post position each time"—and they'll constantly change trainers or the types of races the horse will run in. In fact, they'll do just about anything other than admit that their animal is slow.

Sometimes—whether we're talking about new ideas or racehorses—things don't work out. If that's the case, accept that fact and move on.

When do you know it's time to quit? There are always extremely clear signs:

1. You run out of money . . . and you have no choice.
2. There are no repeat orders, or extremely high returns. Without repeat business, you can't stay in business very long.
3. A new competitor, with a similar or better product, comes on the scene, and the only way you can compete with them is on price.
4. You decide you want to do something else, a decision that could be based on 1, 2, or 3.

FOUR TAKEAWAYS FROM THIS CHAPTER

1. **Study the other guys.** The most effective form of research is to observe what the competition is doing and then do it differently; better, cheaper, or faster.

2. **Count your chips before you begin.** If you only have a limited amount of money, you need to concentrate on developing new products and services in the area where you can get the biggest return the fastest.

3. **Get out into the marketplace as quickly as you can.** It's the only way you can really tell if you're truly on to something.

4. **Don't stay too long.** As Kenny Rogers once sang, "Know when to hold 'em and know when to fold 'em." If your idea isn't working, and it can't be fixed (at a reasonable cost and within a reasonable amount of time), accept that and move on to something else.

There Is No Sense Making a Mistake Unless You Can Learn from It

We all make mistakes, and I've probably made more than most. It doesn't matter if we're talking about my personal life (when I was young and did not get good grades in school), or when I was older in business (see our discussion back in Principle 2), I've made a lot of mistakes.

I think that's a good thing.

If you never want to make a mistake, then don't do anything. If you always play it safe—research, double- and triple-check everything before you move an inch—then you probably won't make many mistakes.

You probably won't accomplish much, either.

To be successful, you can't remain cautious; you must take calculated risks. If you're going to take calculated risks, you're going to make mistakes.

What's important is to learn from them, so that you can actually end up benefiting from those mistakes. It sounds obvious, but it's not what most people do. They will fail at something, and yes, they will take steps to make sure that they don't fail again, but let's look at two steps they usually take.

1. Going forward, they'll make sure they won't make the same mistake again. For example, early in their career they were criticized for misspellings, incorrect names, and missing several commas in a PowerPoint presentation. So, for the rest of their life they triple-check their work and always

have two other people proofread all their presentations. As a result, they spend more time making sure that everything is spelled correctly than they do actually giving quality advice.

2. They simply avoid the situation altogether. For example, back when they were in their midtwenties, they gave a speech and it didn't go well. So, for the rest of their career, they avoid situations where they have to speak in public. Sure sounds to me like they are shrinking their world and becoming overly cautious. (Not surprisingly, their career suffers.)

Neither of these paths are the ones you want to take. As I said, you want to learn from your failures so you can build off of them.

Here's a personal example. When I was young, I was a bit cocky and so I didn't always make the best decisions. I didn't study for my Certified Public Accountant exam, even though I knew for a fact that it's more difficult than the certification that lawyers take (and almost every lawyer takes a review course before they sit for the bar exam). Not surprisingly, I didn't pass.

Well, I could have taken either of the several paths we just talked about. I could've said I would take a CPA review course—which everyone says is the best way to prepare—or I could have simply not taken the test again and found something else to do with my master's in taxation rather than become a CPA.

Neither path would have helped me learn from my mistake. My mistake was that I didn't study. I needed to figure out the best way to study. (The second option wasn't a possibility. I really wanted the CPA designation.)

Well, it's true that review courses work best for most people. I tried one of them, and again I failed the test. I've never really learned well that way. I looked at myself in the mirror and asked myself, "Where is my core competency?" The answer was that I have an uncanny ability to "see patterns" and this helps me solve problems.

> Obviously, you're going to make mistakes. The question is: What are you going to do the next time?

So, the best thing for me to do was to get hold of the five previous CPA exams—they were legally and readily available—and to start studying them. Not only was I looking to see the right answers, I wanted to know how much emphasis they were putting on theory and how much on specific areas like tax, accounting, and ethics. I discovered there were patterns as to which types of questions and subject areas might appear on the next exam. As a result of poring over the previous tests, I passed the next CPA exam with ease.

You always want to learn from your mistakes so you can put that knowledge to your advantage in the future. Again, it ties back to the whole concept of being a calculated risk-taker.

> Look for patterns and gain a competitive advantage!

If you eliminate mistakes, you improve your chances of being successful next time. And if you eliminate the mistakes and then capitalize on that learning, you tip the odds even further in your favor.

You always want to minimize the risks you face and maximize the opportunities.

I like sports analogies, so let me use one from golf to underscore the point. The way every golf course in the world is laid out, the expectation is you'll take two putts, once you're on the green, to get the ball into the hole.

Suppose you're not a great putter and you average two and a half putts per eighteen holes. That means you're taking nine more shots than you should, per round.

If you can correct that and get it down to two putts per hole, you will reduce your handicap by nine. (Instead of shooting 100 as you usually do, you're down to averaging 91.)

> Mistakes—if you treat them correctly—really are an opportunity. This isn't a platitude. It's a fact.

Let's say you really studied what you had been doing wrong: Your balance was off and you were holding the putter too tightly. You kept working at your putting, to the point it's now the strongest part of your game. Instead of taking two putts per green, you are averaging 1.75 putts. All of sudden, you're posting very respectable scores of 86 or 87.

CASE STUDY: LEARNING FROM ONE OF THE CLASSIC MISTAKES OF ALL TIME, THE EDSEL

"There's a commonly held belief that the Edsel was somehow horrible, that it was shoddily built or in some way hideous. These beliefs, though not entirely groundless, fall well short of telling the whole story of why the Edsel failed." This is the way Jacob Joseph begins his analysis on CarBuzz.com to describe what is commonly cited as one of the biggest mistakes of all time.

In fact, the Ford Motor Company didn't make one mistake in manufacturing and introducing the Edsel; it made many. It began with the decision to create the car in the first place.

As Anthony Young wrote in *Automobile Quarterly*, "Ford executives attributed General Motors' large market share [at the time] to GM's wide range of offerings—from the low-priced Chevrolet and Pontiac, to the mid-priced Buick and Oldsmobile, up to the luxury-priced Cadillac. Henry Ford II and Board Chairman Ernest Breech believed that the low-priced Ford, upper-middle-priced Mercury and luxury-priced Lincoln car lines left a gap Ford should fill."

That, in and of itself, may not have been wrong, but how Ford decided to fill the perceived gap certainly was. The initial plan was to have Lincoln-Mercury dealers sell the Edsel, but at the last minute the decision was made for Edsel to be a freestanding division. One of the many problems was that the car would still be built at Lincoln-Mercury and Ford plants where "every 61st car down the Ford or Mercury assembly line was an Edsel. Workers had to reach for parts in separate bins, mistakes were made and quality suffered," Young writes.

And that was just the beginning of the problems.

- The company made the decision that the car should have a dramatic front grill to stand out in the marketplace. By the time the committee appointed to design it finished, it was variously described as "an Oldsmobile sucking a lemon," "a horse collar," and even "a toilet seat."
- Given the long lead time in producing the car, Ford kept up a steady stream of "leaks" to the press to keep the public interested in the "car of the future." All this publicity set up extremely high expectations, expectations that would have been virtually impossible to meet.
- Then there was the matter of the name. Ford's legendary ad agency Foote, Cone & Belding initially came up with eight thousand potential names and winnowed the list down to ones like Pacer, Ranger, and Corsair. The Ford Executive Committee couldn't decide and in "exasperation," as Young put it, Chairman Breech said "Why don't we just call it Edsel?" Edsel Ford was Henry Ford's only son. Edsel's three sons, William Clay, Benson, and Henry II, were all opposed to Breech's suggestion, but the name was adopted. Twelve months of work to come up with just the right name was wasted. In a terse memo, the public relations direc-

tor for the new division, C. Gayle Warnock, typed, "We have just lost 200,000 sales."

But the "real problem with the Edsel was that it was confusing," Joseph writes. "Ford was never really able to define exactly what the hell it was or why you would want one. The Edsel range of vehicles were more or less slotted in between the Ford and Mercury brands, but the company didn't really do a very good job of making this positioning clear. Low-end Edsel models cost about the same as a top-end Ford, which would've been fine if there was some sort of reason for the extra cost, but it wasn't really clear what that reason was, and the fully-loaded Ford was clearly the better deal. Pricier Edsel models cost as much or more than comparable Mercury models, but didn't offer any kind of reason why you should pick one over the other.

"Even before the first model year was up, Edsel sales and marketing were folded into the Lincoln-Mercury division, where they were ignored and left to die."

EXERCISE 11: **THE EDSEL**

1. Was the Edsel truly needed in the marketplace?

2. If you said no, what would you have done to counter GM's dominance? If you said yes, how would you have positioned the vehicle?

3. Was a freestanding division a good idea executed poorly, or simply a bad decision?

4. What role should the Ford Executive Committee have played? (Remember that the Ford Company, at that time, was very much a family business.)

YOU HAVE TO ADMIT YOUR MISTAKES

You've seen this situation hundreds of times. (You may, in fact, have been the main character yourself at least once.) You work incredibly hard to develop a great product or service. You introduce it into the marketplace . . . and it bombs.

Your reaction? "The problem wasn't me or my product. The problem was the market/customer/whoever didn't appreciate what I had. It was a great product (or service). The customers are idiots. That's all there is to it." Because you are convinced you are right and everyone else is wrong, no learning takes place after the fact. There is nothing to learn, you argue. You did everything right.

Written down this way, it sounds silly, doesn't it?

The only person who gets to decide whether you have a truly great product is the customer. If they love it, you do. If they don't, you don't. If they don't buy what you are trying to sell them, you need to figure out why. Otherwise, you run the very real risk of making the same mistake next time.

Now, you could be right. It could've been a great product, but it might have been one that solved no real need. Or maybe it solved a need, but you didn't communicate it clearly enough. Or maybe it solved a need and the communication was good, but . . .

I love competing against people who don't learn from their mistakes.

If you've studied their patterns, you know exactly what they're going to do in any situation—because they always do the same thing—and it's easy to take advantage of that fact. It's like playing poker with people who constantly show you all their cards.

You need to figure out what the problem was. Make no mistake, there was a problem. Otherwise, the product would have sold. Figure out what went wrong and learn from it.

ONE WAY OF REDUCING MISTAKES AHEAD OF TIME

Obviously, it would be better not to make mistakes. That's not possible. One way to reduce the number you and your staff are going to commit is to be extremely clear on expectations up front.

As an employee, you want to know whether the person you're working for only wants "textbook" answers, or really wants solutions that are outside the norm and might be more effective than usual. (Your boss will fall into either of these two camps.)

If you're hiring people, you need to tell them whether you want things strictly by the book, or whether you want them to also use unconventional approaches to get the best answers.

Knowing the approach that is expected will make everyone's life easier.

LET OTHERS HELP YOU LEARN

As you analyze what went wrong, have others help you. If they were part of the decision-making that led to the mistake, they may have insights (and the process of analyzing what went wrong will help them learn as well). If they were not part of the initial decision, they may be able to see things with fresh eyes.

There is a tendency for senior leaders not to involve others in their after-the-fact analysis. Part of this, I believe, is that they simply don't think to do it. Another reason is probably that, somehow, they think they're going to be criticized and blamed for the mistake.

Well, the leader is always ultimately responsible, so that's not a very good reason for not involving others. The reality is that you should not take it personally; you're all just trying to come up with better solutions together.

YOU CAN LEARN FROM OTHER PEOPLE'S MISTAKES BY OBSERVING THEIR PATTERNS

I love reading biographies. I look for ideas that I can borrow and use in my own life. You know, if George S. Patton typically did X, Y, and Z and was successful, then maybe if I do those three things I will be successful too. I'm also interested in how people do things differently. Steve Jobs is an example of using both positive and negative reinforcement.

Jobs frequently would call his employees or suppliers "idiots" or worse when they gave him less than an A+ answer or turned in less than A+ work. What I noticed in reading his biography was that denigrating people could have two effects.

There were some who found this criticism devastating and never recovered. Clearly, it was a mistake to try to motivate those people that way.

But for others, it was a motivating force; they were driven to show Jobs that he was wrong and that they were capable of doing great work. After being criticized, they went back, tried even harder, and excelled.

For example, when Jobs wanted to use glass in his iPhone, he went to Corning to see if they could manufacture it for Apple. The president of Corning explained to Jobs that it couldn't be done from a technology point of view. Jobs told him "to get his arms around it and find a way to do it; if you can't, you shouldn't be president."

Six months later, Corning was producing the Gorilla Glass that Apple needed for the phone.

When the business is facing difficult times, I believe motivating people to work harder is essential; if the "carrot doesn't work, use the stick."

A CHECKLIST THAT CAN HELP YOU REDUCE YOUR MISTAKES

The book is long out of print, which is too bad, but in *Getting It Right the Second Time*, Michael Gershman came up with a wonderful checklist that you can use after something has failed to help you figure out why.

Yes, of course, every failure is caused by different reasons. But invariably, if something went wrong, he says it can be attributed to one of the following reasons:

1. **Perception.** People simply didn't understand what you wanted the product or service to be. (See our discussion of the Edsel earlier in the chapter.)

2. **Pitch.** You stressed the wrong product attributes, or did it in the wrong way.

3. **Price.** It was too high, or sometimes (surprisingly) too low.

4. **Packaging.** Was it attractive or did it send the wrong message? (For example, it looked down-market, even though you were trying to sell a high-end product.)

5. **Piggybacking.** Sometimes coming out with a "me too" product is fine when the market, for a certain type of product or service, is exploding. Other times saying, "It works just as well as X" is the wrong way to go. If the price is basically the same, people will go with the original.

6. **Promotion.** Would you really buy a luxury car because it's promoted as being "least expensive in its class"?

7. **Promises.** This one is almost always fatal. If you promise something—or overpromise—and don't deliver, you'll lose the customer forever.

8. **Positioning.** Is what you have the best or the cheapest; just as good as the leading brand at half the price? You need to make your positioning both explicit and appropriate for your product. 7-Up was a struggling soft drink before it began to position itself as "the Uncola."

9. **Placement.** Was the product in the right stores—and in the right position within the store? If you're selling a high-end toy, you may not want to be in Toys "R" Us. Or would your product be better off near the register than down an aisle?

10. **Premium.** Cracker Jack was just another failing snack food until they hit on the idea of including a "prize" (premium) in every package.
11. **Publicity.** Did you get the word out? Effectively?
12. **Perseverance.** Did you give up too soon?
13. **Procedure.** If you have a certain way of doing things, did you follow it in the case of your failure? If you always have three senior people sign off on an idea, for example, did they, in this instance?

FOUR TAKEAWAYS FROM THIS CHAPTER

1. **Be willing to make mistakes if you want to be successful.** Doing the same thing over and over again may be safe, but you rarely grow if you take that route. You should continue to take calculated risks.

2. **Let the marketplace tell you whether you are right.** It's great that you think you have the best product in the world, but if no one buys it, you don't. Put another way, if the dogs won't eat the dog food, it's bad dog food no matter what you think.

3. **Analyze your mistakes.** Always get input from other people. They may see things you don't.

4. **Don't forget to learn from the mistakes of others.** They can keep you from making the same mistake yourself.

What Is the Most Effective Tool to Solve a Problem or Deal with a Crisis? SWOT

The most effective way, I have found, to answer the question in this chapter title, is to do a SWOT analysis. (In a minute, you'll see modifications I made to make it more effective.)

SWOT is an acronym. When you face a challenge or a new opportunity, ask yourself questions in the following four categories:

■ **Strengths.** What resources can I bring to the situation? How can I capitalize on the unique abilities that I (and my company) are good at to either turn the challenge around or minimize the problem?

■ **Weaknesses.** You think you have an idea that can give you an edge. What are the flaws in your thinking?

■ **Opportunities.** Is there something here that you can turn to your advantage, that you could capitalize on to give you a competitive edge? What can you do better and/or differently than your competition?

■ **Threats.** Where are you vulnerable? You've already identified the weaknesses in your position; now you want to know how those weaknesses could hurt you. How could the competition take advantage of them? How could they damage you long term?

There are numerous advantages of going through a SWOT analysis. Specifically, it can:

1. Help you resolve the challenge(s) you face.
2. Help chart an efficient course of action.
3. Provide you with more data so you can make better decisions.
4. Keep you from making the same mistakes again. (You can see why I have put this chapter after the previous one).

A SWOT analysis can reduce the chances of something going wrong and increase your chances for success, which is always a good thing. One way to do that is to call on your advisory board and have them give you honest feedback in the form of a SWOT assessment. They will look at the same situation you're examining and, hopefully, identify weaknesses and threats you haven't noticed.

For example, you've come up with an absolutely brilliant (you're convinced) new product and initial testing is through the roof. They might ask you, "How are you going to get the independent distributors to carry it?"

Questions like this may seem like they create a roadblock, but they really don't. You're going to have to deal with weaknesses and threats eventually—the marketplace is going to force you to—so you might as well address them before you launch your product or service. On a brighter note, your board and employees should be able to highlight additional strengths and opportunities. They should also provide you with new ideas and approaches. If you are not confident that your board and/or your employees can do a SWOT effectively, or you think they will only tell you what you want to hear, have an outsider do the SWOT analysis with them. But no matter what approach you take, make sure you do it.

SWOT BY THE NUMBERS

SWOT is all about identifying strengths, weaknesses, opportunities, and threats. How many items in each category should you have?

My answer: At least five. There are a couple of reasons for this.

First, you need to take the exercise seriously. If you have fewer than five, you're going to be tempted to dash off the first two or three thoughts that come to mind and say you're done.

Second, you may only list the threats and weaknesses you have a terrific answer for. A longer list will keep you honest.

Sometimes, when I say you need at least five, people come back and say, "I can't come up with that many."

My answer is always the same: "Think harder."

SWOT AND TIME

Most people use SWOT to create a snapshot in time. Here are the strengths, weaknesses, opportunities, and threats we face as of today. That's fine, but if you only do what everyone else does, you're never going to beat them; you'll only tie. Remember that the reason we're doing the SWOT analysis in the first place is to gain a competitive advantage.

This is why I suggest you also use SWOT to help you project where you and your company are going to be five years out. Which threats that are small now could become larger ones in a few years? Conversely, which potential opportunities could become huge?

The nice thing about doing this is that it forces you to balance short-term and long-term goals and bring real-world market forces into play. For example, your SWOT analysis might look one way if you know the goal is to grow the company. It might look completely different if you are looking to sell within five years.

You always have short-term and long-term threats and opportunities. That's why you want to always use SWOT over both time frames.

In a funny way, doing a five-year SWOT analysis can substitute for the business plans I hate. A business plan can give you a false sense of security, because you're doing the financial projections virtually in a vacuum and you can make the numbers do whatever you like. ("Hmmm, looks like sales will be a little low in year four. You know, if we assume that they're going to be 2% higher—and how hard can it be to obtain that—we should be all right.")

The SWOT analysis, if you are candid, will keep you honest.

CASE STUDY: BODY ARMOR

Imagine you wanted to start a company that manufactures a concealable, bulletproof vest. Your goals are to make a vest that is "the absolute best."

EXERCISE 12: BODY ARMOR

1. How do you determine what the vest should look like and what characteristics it should have?

2. How would you fill in the four quadrants of the SWOT analysis? (Make sure you have at least five entries per quadrant, and document your answers in detail.)

3. How will examining competitors and different industries provide you with a competitive advantage?

4. What imaginative way would you advertise your product?

5. What is the key ingredient of the vest that will make it successful?

SWOT AS AN INVESTMENT TOOL

When he was asked for investment advice, Malcolm S. Forbes, the man who turned the magazine his father started into the well-respected business publication it is today, would always reply, "Bet on the jockey and not the horse." His meaning was clear: It's more important to invest in a good leader than a good idea. You can always tweak the idea; changing someone's fundamental character is more difficult.

I agree. When deciding if I should hire someone or invest in a company I'm interested in, I try to get as much information as I can about the person or company beforehand so I can get a "feel" for them. Then, I always put their idea—or how they think—under the SWOT microscope, and it's really interesting to see what's revealed.

A FINAL THOUGHT ABOUT THIS

People don't use SWOT analysis as often as I think they should. There are a couple of reasons why they don't.

People don't like to do it because it forces them to confront weaknesses and threats. They think, somehow, that if they work hard enough examining a market, they can eliminate everything that possibly could go wrong, or by admitting a potential problem it'll make them look ineffective. Both these things are just silly. You should not be looking at this as an exercise designed to make you look bad. Rather, it's intended to maximize your company's performance.

Other people don't take the exercise seriously enough. They think if they write the first three things they can think of in each category, they're done. They're just trying to check an item off the list, instead of using SWOT to find a true competitive advantage. You undertake a SWOT analysis because you want to have the greatest potential to make the most money. That isn't going to happen unless you have identified all four quadrants in detail.

When I say you, I really mean everyone in the company. Everyone who works with you should be able to use this tool effectively.

FOUR TAKEAWAYS FROM THIS CHAPTER

1. **SWOT is not as popular a tool as it should be.** It will give you an advantage over your competitors if you use it.

2. **Prioritize.** While business plans are basically useless, a SWOT analysis, done correctly, crystallizes the real business issues that you face.

3. **Work hard.** Make sure you have at least five well-considered thoughts in each of the strengths, weaknesses, opportunities, and threats boxes.

4. **Double check.** Ask your advisory board and employees to double-check your work. Not only may they come up with weaknesses and threats that you may have overlooked, but they could identify strengths and opportunities that you might have missed.

If It Ain't Broke—Break It.

Don't Be Complacent.

Always Improve. Always Get Better.

The advice in the title doesn't immediately win me friends among people who've built successful companies. If you imagine yourself in their position, you'll understand why.

There you are, finally making money—maybe even a great deal of money—after putting in eighty- ninety- or hundred-hour weeks for years trying to get your company up and running. You'd like to slow down a bit, maybe only work sixty or seventy hours a week, and have the chance to sneak away on the occasional Friday afternoon to play golf. And here I am saying, "Your company can't afford to become lax. You need to be constantly working to stay ahead of the competition and making sure you're anticipating your customers' needs."

Sheesh.

Well the fact of the matter is, you can never become complacent. Sure, things are fine now, but:

■ Things change. The economy gets hot, or cools off, and your company has to respond accordingly.

■ Not only do new competitors enter the marketplace, but existing competitors get better.

■ Computers and apps now allow the business world to operate at "warp speed." As a result, new products and new ways of disseminating information are being created faster than ever before.

■ Customers' needs and wants evolve as well—invariably they want more and better, and to pay less. (If you ask them if they want higher quality and/or lower prices, they're always going to say "yes.")

The result of all this requires you to change and evolve—quickly. Otherwise, someone—maybe one of my students—is going to come and take away everything you've earned with a cheaper, faster, and/or improved version of what you're offering today. (In other words, they're going to do to you what you did to someone else when you were first getting under way.)

> You should always anticipate what your customers' future needs will be before they ask for it.

There's another important reason you need to keep evolving rapidly. Many of our nation's schools, including some business schools (not Babson), teach that the world is a predictable place. So they assume that studying what worked in the past will prepare you for the future. That's simply not the case, as a quick glance at the papers will prove. Traditional formal planning just doesn't work. The world—especially the business world for entrepreneurs—is just not that predictable.

If you assume that tomorrow things will be pretty much like today, you will end up reacting to changes in the marketplace and playing "catch-up." Conversely, if you're always trying to figure out how to get better, you'll stay on offense instead of constantly playing defense. All this explains why your company has to be continually scanning for weaknesses and threats and looking for places where you can build on your strengths and take advantage of opportunities.

But just because your company has to do this, it doesn't mean you have to be the one doing it. You can delegate this task of staying ahead of the competition, provided you truly empower your people to take advantage of what they learn through constantly doing the SWOT analysis we talked about in the last chapter.

You are entitled to slow down a bit. In fact, I think it's a good idea. It's not that you can't keep putting in those seventy-, eighty-, and ninety-hour weeks. You could, physically; but mentally, especially if you have achieved some success, it begins to wear on you and then you begin (if only subconsciously) longing to take it a bit easier. Then, you do (at least subconsciously), and things begin to fall through the cracks, as you start saying for the first time, "I'll deal with that tomorrow [or next week]." You lose your edge . . . and your company does as well.

> People who don't watch the competition get complacent.
> The graveyards are filled with complacent companies.

So, by all means, start easing up a bit. Just make sure someone else is keeping an eye on the competition and making sure that your company is constantly improving.

WHAT WE ARE TALKING ABOUT BREAKING

It has always surprised me: when I tell people, "If it ain't broke, break it," they think I'm suggesting blowing up every part of their organization on a regular basis. I'm not. In fact, what I'm advocating could keep you from having to do that.

The only time you completely want to revamp your entire company is when you have no choice—like when it is threatened and may go out of business.

If you're constantly improving and constantly getting better, you can avoid this situation, unless there's a radical shift in technology or in the way business is done. (You could've been making the world's best manual typewriters and doing everything right when it came to constantly improving, but once word processers came along you were in a lot of trouble.) Unless you are upended by that kind of seismic change, continuous improvement should hold you in good stead.

As you've already guessed, what I'm advocating is constantly making small tweaks.

Here's how it works in my companies. Because this approach is so engrained, we begin this process each year in September. We sit down and examine which of our products are selling well and which aren't.

When it comes to the laggards, we identify the bottom 25%, the quarter of our products that have the slowest sales growth, lowest margins, or both. Then, since we have said throughout that there are no real failures if you learn from them, we look to see why the products underperformed. In some cases, improvements are relatively easy to come by: better packaging might do the trick, improving the offering, or repositioning it as "new and improved" could be the way to go.

In some instances, about 10% to 15% of the time, it's time for the product to be retired. Consumers have grown tired of it, or the competition has a better version that we just can't match.

However, this represents a huge opportunity, because we already have the shelf space and distribution to handle our products. Let's say we have a hundred products. By cutting ten to fifteen, we have opened up ten to fifteen slots that we can fill.

Constantly performing a SWOT analysis keeps someone from sneaking up on you.

In fact, continually improving is similar to the Act. Learn. Build. Repeat. model that we discussed in Principle 4.

You'll remember, the key component of step one—Act—is taking a small smart step toward your goals. It's no different here. You begin with small steps. Maybe you begin at the edges. You try a new product or service on a limited scale, in a test market, and learn from the market reaction. Or maybe you decide you'll start at your core, with an "add-on" product or service, and see what people think. For example, you aren't risking much, and you aren't in danger of confusing people, if you offer a diet version of the soft drink you're currently selling, or the "professional" version of your software.

As you can see, what we're doing here is tying the Act. Learn. Build. Repeat. model directly to the strategy you want to employ and the financial results you're looking for. Let me end our discussion at this point by stressing this: you're not changing your core products—the regular version of the soft drink or the existing version of the software; you're coming out with additional (enhanced) versions (diet, in the case of the soft drinks; professional, in the case of the software).

If you constantly do this incrementally and do it in anticipation of what customers will want, you're going to make it tougher and tougher for the competition to catch up with you, let alone pass you by. You'll remain relevant—and profitable.

ATTACK ON TWO FRONTS SIMULTANEOUSLY

As you're tweaking what you have, you want to be doing line extensions—diet, new flavors, new diet flavors, bigger portions, smaller portions, etc.—and new products as well. This just makes sense. Building off what you have lets you pick the proverbial low-hanging fruit. Adding new products/services allows you to grow.

> Remember how I said we're always trying to upgrade our staff, getting rid of the bottom-performing 10% each year. It's the same thing here. As you're upgrading your product line, you always want to be getting rid of the worst performers.

There's no template for doing any of this. You keep making small, incremental improvements; pause to see how the market reacts; build off that learning by making another small change and so on, upgrading your overall offerings as you go.

Should you concentrate in one area—improving the core—at the expense of another (i.e., introducing new products)? There is no formula. You generate as many good ideas as you can in both areas and winnow your list down to the absolute best. If it turns out that one year all your best ideas involve improving your core business, that's great. If the next year every promising concept revolves around new products, that's fine, too. You should have no bias in one direction or the other.

COLUMBIA RESTAURANTS

If there were ever a case of where "if it ain't broke, don't fix it" would seem to apply, it would be the Columbia Restaurants in Florida that we mentioned earlier. Famous for their Cuban and Spanish food, the places are always packed with locals, snowbirds, and tourists. Columbia is run by an exceptional entrepreneur, Richard Gonzmart, who has all the qualities I admire in a successful entrepreneur: He is smart, hardworking, innovative, a calculated risk-taker, and extremely charitable.

As of this writing, Richard, a fourth-generation owner, is planning to open even more restaurants. Each of the new locations has a chance to energize and improve what's already in place.

Here are some examples. Up until now, all of Columbia's eateries were destination restaurants where you could plan on spending an hour or two dining. Richard opened a fast-service place in Tampa International Airport, called Columbia Restaurant Café. Not only will this remind visitors to the area of the Columbia brand as they're coming and going, the most popular offerings from all his other restaurants could find their way onto the lunch menus under a special section for people looking for "a quick lunch." (Not everyone gets a full hour to eat in the middle of the day.)

One of his projects that has now come to fruition is a restaurant in St. Petersburg. It has a gorgeous view of the water, and a huge bar—far bigger than what exists in any of his other places—that serves tapas. Not only are the margins higher on liquor than food, but the focus on alcohol and snacks attracts a younger crowd. The demographics of the traditional Columbia Restaurants tend to skew older.

While proving that he's not abandoning his roots, Gonzmart has opened a unique riverside restaurant in a newly developed area of Tampa. Once the home of many Native Americans, Tampa is the city where the first Columbia Restaurant opened. The restaurant, called Ulele (pronounced You-lay-lee) is named for the daughter of a legendary Native American chief. The menu includes native and local foods and it has its own brewery. He has also acquired the rights to the restaurant Goody Goody Burgers—a place Richard enjoyed eating at when he was young and living in Tampa. The restaurant had closed in 2005. Richard recently brought it back to life.

When asked why he is doing all this, Richard reacts exactly as you would expect, saying that if you're not growing, you're dying, and you need to stay ahead of the competition. He adds, "Sometimes, it's just fun to try new things."

Is there an alternative to doing all this?

After I run through everything we have talked about so far, some people respond, "It sure sounds like a lot of work. Are you certain I have to do all this?"

The answer is: you don't.

"What will happen if I don't?" is always the follow-up question.

You'll end up looking a lot like Xerox PARC.

Most of you know the history. Xerox, once the dominant player in photocopying, set up the Palo Alto Research Center (PARC) in 1970 to spur innovation in the company. It certainly did. Its scientists and engineers created many of the products and ideas that serve as the backbone of computing today, everything from Ethernet to the mouse.

However, the company wasn't much interested in capitalizing on those literally revolutionary concepts and let others—notably Apple—run with them. Not surprisingly, Xerox then fell on hard times as other companies cut into their core market.

You can go the route of staying exactly the way you are, but I would not recommend it.

YOU CAN TEACH YOUR PEOPLE TO DO THIS

I'm always surprised that organizations don't introduce this approach company-wide, don't insist that employees at all levels employ the "if it ain't broke, break it" model. On second thought, maybe I shouldn't be surprised, because when they try to do it, invariably they take the wrong approach and botch it.

You know the route they take. They summon everyone with the title of middle manager and above to an "all-hands meeting where we'll discuss the future of our organization." At the meeting, people are encouraged to suggest ideas on "how we can reinvent our company."

I have found that, in many cases, the middle-and senior-level managers sitting there consider this meeting to be a serious waste of time. They have no authority to change anything this sweeping, so they suggest a couple of things off the top of their heads and go back to what they consider to be their real jobs.

No wonder this never works.

A far better approach is to explain to everyone in the company what the specific objective is. "Five years from now, one-third of our sales needs to be coming from products and services we do not offer today."

Then, since you never want to turn down a good idea, you tell everyone: "If you have ideas for overarching things you think the company can do to reach that goal, please tell us. It might be easier—and more effective—for you to concentrate on telling us what your department can do to help us get there. (Of course, we'll be sharing with you the positive results that come from your suggestions.)"

I have found this approach gets everyone engaged.

FOUR TAKEAWAYS FROM THIS CHAPTER

1. **Waiting until you have to change is not good.** You never want things to get to that point.

2. **You want to be constantly making incremental improvements** to stay ahead of the competition and giving customers what they want (hopefully, before they even know they want it).

3. **The best way of creating and implementing changes** is by constantly performing SWOT analyses.

4. **Do it as a team.** The whole really is greater than the sum of the parts.

Be a Mensch

First things first: Let's deal with the chapter title. Although it sounds like a place for guys to sit while the women they know shop for clothes—that is, the man's bench, or mensch—this isn't what the word means. In Yiddish, it means "a good person," someone who has qualities you would hope for in a close friend or colleague.

This is how you should behave in business. You should be a mensch.

I suppose that comment isn't surprising coming from someone who once thought he would become a rabbi. I realized early on that you cannot follow one set of rules while reading the Torah—the Bible—and another as you live the rest of your life. You either practice what you believe in, or you don't.

It's a lesson I learned growing up watching my dad, Abram Green. A&P was his largest customer and one day, during a period when his business was struggling, A&P paid Dad twice by mistake. A&P sent Dad a check for $35,000, paying for goods that it had previously paid for.

Some of Dad's employees told him to keep the money. "They are a big company," they said, "They'll never miss it."

"It isn't about them," Dad said as he returned the check, "It's about me."

I think that's a good place to begin the discussion, with you and what you believe. What are you totally comfortable doing in your interactions with others? How do you want to live your business life when it comes to morals, ethics, and doing the right thing? Do you want to be a mensch?

When I ask this, people instantly respond, "You don't under-stand. If I always do what you say, I'm going be exploited. Not ev-eryone thinks this way, and they'll take advantage of me."

When they say this, I tell them I understand completely. I then explain to them what happened to me back when I attended Rutgers University. I never had a car, but I was getting serious about my then girlfriend, Lois (Lois Green, my wife of fifty-plus years), and I fi-nally decided that I was going to get a car. One of my fraternity brothers sold me a car he had refurbished. The first time I took it out, Lois and I had not gone more than two blocks when the engine literally fell out.

When I confronted my fraternity brother, all he said was, "Wel-come to the real world, Lenny Green."

So I understand that people may try to take advantage of you, but you can choose whether or not you take advantage of them. I know I can only control certain things, but I have chosen not to take advantage of others. This is a lesson I try to get across every year in class.

Each year, I give a hypothetical problem that involves the stu-dents having to make an ethical decision on whether they want to cheat to be successful or whether they will remain ethical. Every year the majority decides to be ethical.

Then, unbeknownst to them I give them a real-world problem.

Earlier in the semester, I asked Woody Lappen, the man who for twenty-five years has run one of the concessions on the Babson campus, to come in and talk about his business. (Woody is a classic entrepreneur.)

A couple of weeks later, Woody walks into my classroom and in-terrupts the class.

"I am sorry, Professor," Woody says. "Would you mind terribly if I leave these fifty slushies at the back of the room? There is a fac-ulty meeting here right after your class, and I want to surprise the professors."

I tell him it wasn't a problem and return to teaching my class. About ten minutes later, I walk over to the slushies and say, "These sure look good. I'm not going to the faculty meeting—in fact, the meeting is for another department entirely—but he did say the slushies were a surprise. The professors will never know if I have one, so I think I will."

I take a sip and say, "Gee, these really are great. Does anybody else want to have one?" A couple of the students raise their hands, and I give one to each of them. They, too, rave about the drinks and a few more students ask for one, and then a few more, and before you know it, all the slushies are gone.

Just before the class ends, I ask the students if they think what we did—drinking all the slushies—was wrong. We get into a debate about whether or not it was, and then I reveal something that you might have guessed.

"I asked Woody to bring the slushies into class. I paid for them. They weren't a surprise for the teachers. There is no faculty meeting. This was a test to see what you would do when faced with a real situation, not a hypothetical case study. I wanted to reinforce the lesson of ethical business behavior that we talked about before."

This triggers another round of discussion with many of the students saying that on their own they wouldn't have taken a slushie, but once they saw me do it, they figured it was okay.

This brings up a couple of points. First, it really shouldn't matter what anyone else does; you are ultimately responsible for deciding between right and wrong for yourself. You want to be able to face the person staring back in the mirror.

Secondly, saying that is a bit naïve on my part. Of course people are going to watch what the leader—me in this case—does. His actions always speak far louder than his words. The head person sets the tone for everything in a company, and people can easily justify dishonest behavior by saying, in this case, "If Len did it, it is okay." People can rationalize anything.

What that means is if you're the leader, you need to model the behavior you want from your employees. This modeling extends to showing the rest of the organization how you're going to treat employees who are unethical. In my case, I fire them. We have a zero tolerance policy in this regard in my company.

I know, many think this is an overreaction. They tell me that the punishment should fit the crime. If you fudge your time sheets (put in for a few more hours than you actually worked), I should just make you repay the money; and if you ever do it again, *then* you're fired. Alternatively, I could also have you contribute an amount equal to what you overstated to charity. That way, you have to repay twice what you took.

These alternatives have merit, but that isn't the approach I have chosen to take. I don't think there are a lot of shades of gray. If you cheat a customer or our company, you are fired. If your supervisor knew, or should have known about it, he or she is fired too.

You're trying to create a certain culture. You want everyone in your organization to know what you and your firm stand for. Firing people does that. So does giving people paid time off to volunteer for community or charitable projects and "encouraging" people to give back.

HOW YOU SHOULD DEAL WITH OTHERS

Now, just because you're always trying to do the right thing—and are making sure that your people do the right thing as well—it doesn't mean you need to tie one hand behind your back when you're negotiating with others. For example, it's more than fair to put yourself and your product or service in the best possible light.

I'm also a big believer in how the late Roger Fisher, the Harvard professor who wrote the best-selling book on negotiation, *Getting to Yes*, says you should handle a business transaction. He advocates always being honest and answering forthrightly every question put to you. He also says you need not do more than that. If someone doesn't ask you about something, you don't have to tell that person. If there's a flaw in her reasoning—she's undervaluing something that you know should sell for far more, for example—you don't need to point it out.

However, I probably will if it's someone I have an ongoing rela-tionship with. I'll want to be fair and hope my approach is reciprocated. I go into every business transaction wanting to believe the person I'm dealing with will be honest and aboveboard. However, I'm always prepared for them not to be.

> Shame on me if I believe everyone is going to be honest—but I would like to start there.

A quick story will make the point. Early in my career, I did a lot of sale-leasebacks of shopping centers. The owners of the entire shopping centers or the anchor store, looking to cash out on their investment, would sell the property to me, and, as part of the deal, they would agree to rent the property back from me at a fixed price for a number of years. (This guaranteed a return on the money I put up.)

Well, the owner in a particular shopping center said he was willing to sell at substantially below market rates because he was strapped for cash.

"That's the only reason?" I asked.

"Yes."

Now, admitting you're in a bad financial position during negotiations is never a good ploy (unless you're being disingenuous). So I decided to dig a little deeper. I had visited the shopping center previously on numerous occasions and knew it was located on a busy highway. The foot traffic appeared to be what the owner said it was, and the existing leases of the other stores in the shopping center were just as represented. Just to make sure I wasn't missing anything, I hired a helicopter so we could literally get a birds'-eye view of the surrounding area. Sure enough, we spotted a problem almost immediately. The state was building a new highway that would siphon off a significant portion of the traffic that went by the center.

We were still scheduled to close on the deal, and I showed up at the appointed hour.

"You know, I was thinking about your financial position," I began. "I hate to take advantage of someone when he's down. I'd like to raise my offer to what the property is actually worth."

"If you want to pay more, I'm certainly not going to object," the seller said.

"I didn't think you would," I said, "but before I do, look me in the eye and tell me there are no problems you haven't disclosed."

"There aren't," he said, staring right at me.

"So you don't think the fact that a new highway is being built and that it's going to reroute 80% of the traffic is a problem?"

> Trust, but verify.

The seller didn't say a word. He just gathered up his papers and left the room. That was the end of the deal—and our relationship.

Was I surprised he was trying to pull "a fast one"? No. Some people are just wired that way. Why do people do things like this? It could be because of the Maslow hierarchy and they need to make the deal happen to survive, or it could be that they think that business is a game without any rules, so they believe they have to be cutthroat at all times. Or it could be that they simply have to win at all costs.

> When I go into a deal, I'm always expecting that the other person will do something (unethical) that I wouldn't do.

Their motivation doesn't matter. You just need to guard against their actions. For reinforcement of this principle, you should read a few accounts of how Bernie Madoff defrauded friends, relatives, charities, and countless others.

THE BENEFITS OF BEING GOOD

Can I say, with absolute certainty, that there are tangible financial payoffs from what I am advocating? No, I can't quantify the numbers. Am I convinced that it has contributed to my success? Yes.

It isn't hard to explain why.

For many years I've done real estate deals with someone, and all he required was a handshake. The legal work followed thereafter, and the legal documents were exactly as the deal had been described it would be. The man, Larry Kadish, is one of the most successful real estate people I have ever met.

However, there was one deal, unbeknownst to Larry, where the tenant, who leased the entire building, went bankrupt just as we closed. As a result, I owned a building with no tenant. I had a real problem, because the value of a property without a tenant was far less than that of a property with a Triple A–rated tenant—which is what I had originally purchased. Larry had no legal obligation to do anything, but he voluntarily substituted a property of equal value.

You can see why Larry and I have been doing business together for over thirty years.

If you have a good working relationship with someone whom you know to be honest and a problem comes up, it'll be fairly easy to resolve. Your supplier says he forgot to charge for part of an order. You can spend ten seconds checking that you haven't been previously billed and then write the check. There is no searching for hidden motives.

If you have trust in one another, you can count on the other person to do the right thing.

CASE STUDY: THE EXOTIC JUICE COMPANY

While the baby-food market is typically dominated by large companies, starting in the 1990s a number of new entrants who emphasized quality products entered the field.

The Exotic Juice Company was founded in the late 1990s, and its
goal was to be the number one quality baby-food juice drink. It
used 100% juice, and its president, the company's spokesman, was
dubbed by the press "Mr. Natural" since the only ingredient in Exotic Juice was "100% natural juice. No additives, no colorings, just
juice," a fact the president said every chance he got when interviewed on radio and TV. Being 100% juice, he said, accounted for
the product's superior taste.

Sales started strong and steadily increased in the company's first
four years. However, since there were no barriers to entry, pretty
soon Exotic Juice found competitors everywhere it looked.

All of a sudden, Exotic Juice started losing money, a lot of money.
A quick look at the cost to produce a bottle of juice shows why this
was the case:

Selling price because of competition	$1.00
Breakdown of Items	**Costs**
100% juice	$0.60
State-of-the-art bottle/packaging	.05
Factory overhead	.25
Marketing and research	.20
SG&A	.15
Total cost	**$1.25**
Loss per bottle	(.25)

If the company didn't do something, it would go out of business.

Since the juice was the most expensive component, one suggestion was for the company to reduce the juice content and substitute
water and sugar. If it used different percentages of juice, the profit
would rise substantially, as reflected below. The taste with the extra
sugar was found to be sweeter and more appealing. Competitors
were using only a percentage of juice in their similar products.

Cost	100% Juice	75% Juice	50% Juice	25% Juice	0% Juice
Juice	$0.60	0.45	0.3	0.15	0
Sugar/water	$0	0.05	0.1	0.15	0.2
Total cost	0.6	0.5	0.4	0.3	0.2
Savings/unit	0	0.1	0.2	0.3	0.4

Note 1: A reduction of 50% of the juice content resulted in a $0.05 profit per bottle.

Note 2: A reduction of 99% of the juice content resulted in a profit of approximately $0.34 a bottle.

EXERCISE 13: **JUICE**

1. Would you reduce the juice content? Zero juice would increase profits by millions of dollars.

2. Would you show the percentage of juice on the label?

3. Would you use "new and improved" on the label?

4. Would you use other strategies to re-invent the company?

FOUR TAKEAWAYS FROM THIS CHAPTER

1. Create a personal mission statement. Just as you have an overall strategy and mission statement for your company, you need to have one for yourself.

2. Follow the Golden Rule. It sounds simplistic, but it's still a good rule of thumb: In the long run, do you want people to treat you the way you treat them?

3. **Remember, cheating isn't winning.** Yes, you want to win, but you want to win the right way.

4. **Understand that ultimately, only you are responsible for your behavior.** You don't get to rationalize it away by saying, "Everyone does it this way," or, "It was okay with my boss." You decide wheter you're going to be a mensch, or you're not.

Ten Steps to Take Before You Make Your Move into Entrepreneurship

The following ten moves can help you to avoid many of the pitfalls first-time entrepreneurs face. Even better, none will cost you a dime.

All you need is a willingness to flex your mind and do some mental research and development—that is, serious thinking.

1. Examine your motives. Being unhappy with your work or wishing you could make more money is not, in itself, necessarily a good reason to become an entrepreneur.

2. Have entrepreneurial characteristics, and know what they are. (List five, and be specific.)

If the five don't easily come to mind, even after reviewing the previous fourteen principles, it isn't fatal. But if you are having trouble picturing yourself as an entrepreneur, recognize that the journey is going to be harder for you than it'll be for other people.

3. Be able to afford losing your investment. You need to acknowledge, before you begin, that this is a possible outcome. It's an understatement to say that not every new venture works out. Can you deal with that, and with the fact that you may lose face before your family and friends if your idea fails?

4. Research the market. Exploring your idea from different angles helps avoid the mistake of creating a product or service that people don't want or won't pay an adequate price for.

5. Narrow the options. It's extremely important to select a business that A) satisfies your personal goals, B) involves the kind of work you like to do and are good at, and C) fits your lifestyle.

6. Test the waters. Although having experience in the business you're starting isn't essential, your chances of success are improved considerably if you do.

7. Build your reputation and credibility today . . . so you will have access to funding when you need it tomorrow. In other words, nurture potential loan and investment sources now so that you won't be stalled by a lack of funds later when you're ready to start.

8. Hone your negotiating skills. Most small businesses survive on the ability of their owners to negotiate with suppliers, salespeople, and the like. One of the best ways to obtain capital is to negotiate and barter for the things you need to get started.

9. Pick the brains of others in the business. You can glean a wealth of practical information on what the business is really like (and whether it's for you) by talking to entrepreneurs in the field you're considering.

10. Take a course in entrepreneurship from a professor who has real world experience. Apply yourself in class to the assignments. Think outside the proverbial box and take calculated risks in seeking unique answers to class assignments.

The beauty of these ten steps is that they will better prepare you to achieve success in the future. They do that by saving you expensive trial-and-error costs, shaving losses you might incur due to lack of knowledge, and steering you into personally and financially satisfying business situations.

EXERCISE 14: **BUSINESS OPPORTUNITIES**

As we have said throughout, to be successful a business must provide a product or service that fills a need. In today's fast-paced and complex society, I have identified multiple areas and niches that require better, quicker, more effective, and less expensive solutions. Can you think of ways to satisfy them? (Fill in the column on the right in the following table. Remember to send me your answers to receive feedback.)

What People Are Asking For	Businesses That Fill That Need
"I need to do everything faster."	
"I need some special service."	
"Help me cope."	
"Tell me only what I need to know."	
"I want to feel and look good."	
"I want reliable service."	
"I want to earn or save money."	
"I want better medical care."	
"I need more training/education."	
"I want more excitement in my life."	

Secrets, Techniques, and Strategies of the Successful Entrepreneurs I Have Worked With

I have been teaching entrepreneurship to CEOs and col-lege students for over twenty-five years, and I have been paid by companies to teach their executives how to be more effective and help their companies become more profitable. Not surprisingly, both the students and executives always ask me for "tips on how to become more successful or to be a better CEO."

I remember reading that when Larry Page returned to Google as CEO, one of the first things he did was to ask Steve Jobs for advice on becoming a "good CEO." Jobs had a rather simple but exact formula that worked for him:

1. Surround yourself with "A players" who are smart.
2. Deliberately have a goal to build a great team.
3. Motivate the team to be better than they think they are.
4. Focus on five products, not a hundred, and produce five great products.
5. Remember the basics—to win, you have to "block and tackle" better than your opposition.
6. Don't get too big or too flabby.
7. Never get too complacent—always be innovative.
8. Never stop learning.

I like Steve's list. Let me add a few ideas of my own, based on what I have learned both throughout my career and by observing other people.

HOW TO CREATE A GREAT TEAM

Developing an effective team is one of the most difficult tasks in business, but it may be one of the most important things any entrepreneur can do. Having a company with good products and good sales is usually not sustainable unless you build an effective team.

New employees usually have ideas for growth and would like to try new things, while the people who've been there for a while think things are just fine the way they are. They are resistant to new ideas and creating new roles. Sounds dysfunctional, doesn't it? It certainly sounds like the employees are pulling in different directions, and it's hard to move forward if that's the case.

One of the most important lessons an entrepreneur needs to learn early on is that he needs to create an effective team if he is ever going to accomplish anything significant. Sure, you could decide to do everything yourself and simply run a micro business. However, as the name implies, it's probably going to be small. To do anything that's going to have significant impact, you'll need to grow, and that means adding employees. In turn, that means getting those employees to work together as a team.

Here's how I do it:

1. To be on my team, you have to be smarter than me. (Many would say this isn't so difficult.)
2. I surround myself with people who are self-motivated.
3. My job is to keep them focused, inspired and to empower them to perform at their best.
4. I try to remove obstacles so they can get their job done without fear of failure.
5. I also try to keep things light with a sense of humor and laughter.

EMPOWERMENT AND LEADING TEAMS

Why go through all this trouble? Because a leader does not have a monopoly on great ideas. You may come up with more than most people, but, most is not all. You want to have as many good ideas as possible, and your teammates can provide you with them.

That's why empowerment of employees is an entrepreneur's secret weapon for success. Your employees may not know how to implement the ideas, and they probably won't have the resources required, but you can help them with all that. What you need are the best ideas and a team of people to carry them out.

Here are the seven steps I try to follow in forming effective teams.

1. **End dysfunction.** It's difficult to build high-performing teams in a dysfunctional environment. People need to feel they're working in a place where they are valued; they know what their role is, and they feel comfortable offering suggestions that will specifically improve their team and the organization in general.

2. **Have great leaders.** I put an "*s*" on "*leader*" for a reason. Yes, of course, there is ultimately one person in charge of the organization, but that doesn't need to be the person running every team. Leaders at all levels need to have knowledge, establish clear goals, and have a passion for the task at hand. They must be the driving force and should lead by example.

> Lee Iacocca said it very well when asked why he hired "eager beavers and mavericks." He replied, "They do more than what is expected of them."

3. **Each of the leaders must have a defined goal.** A true leader knows where they want to go, as opposed to just

saying, "Follow me." It sounds obvious, right? Think about the work teams you have been on. Was that always the case?

4. **Leaders must enjoy seeing people work to their full potential.** They take pride in the fact that members of the team are accomplishing more than they ever thought possible.

5. **Treat people the way you would like to be treated.** That should go without saying, but if you've ever worked within a bad organization, you know this is not common.

6. **Communicate.** First, you'll have to deliver your key messages over and over again. You'll be bored hearing yourself long before the message ever sinks in organization-wide. Second, communicate face-to-face whenever possible; it's simply the best way.

7. **The importance of monitoring.** You'll need regular sessions where you check in on the team's progress and change direction if needed.

 PROOF THIS WORKS

Bob Burton, CEO and chairman of Cenveo, a world leader in commercial printing, custom packaging, envelopes, labels, warehousing fulfillment, and related services, is a great example of someone who does this well. Bob is charismatic and extremely motivated and has an outstanding record of financial success. Before the year begins, company goals are established, and then he holds periodic meetings with all the key executives to monitor their progress. Bob reminds me of many famous football coaches. That's not surprising, since he was an All-American at Murray State and was drafted by the San Francisco 49ers.

HOW TO CREATE A GREAT TEAM (PART II)

We mentioned this earlier, but because it is so important, I want to return to the Maslow hierarchy here.

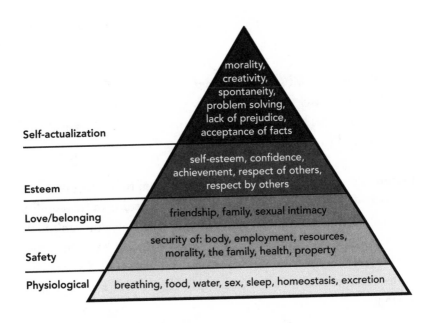

The graphic above is a representation of the work of Abraham Harold Maslow, a psychologist who noticed early on in his career that certain needs take precedence over others. For example, if you're both hungry and thirsty, the need for something to drink will take precedence over eating. This isn't surprising; you can go without food for weeks, but you'll die within days if you don't have something to drink. If you're thirsty and someone is choking you, the desire for air will top your desire for water.

Maslow ranked all needs into five categories; the lower the position in the triangle, the more fundamental the need. For example, as you can see, security is more important than friendship.

Why am I talking about this? It is simple. You can rank the characteristics needed to create effective teams using Maslow's hierarchy. Just like with his triangle, you work from the bottom up.

Physiological. This level is the starting point. What do you look for in team members (something that we'll discuss in a second), and what do you pay them? You can't say people should work for nothing. Even with commissioned salesmen, you need to give them a draw.

Safety. In this context, people want to know where they stand at work, and we tell them.

Love/Belonging. Most people want to do more than trade their time for a paycheck. This is certainly true for people who work at our companies. They like socializing with their coworkers. They look forward to coming to work.

Esteem. People want to do a good job and want to be recognized for doing so. They want to move up the ranks according to their ability, and they don't want to hear there's a rule that says you can't make partner unless you've been here ten years. We don't have these rules and do everything we can to help our people get ahead. We'll pay for professional education classes and give time off to attend training sessions.

Self-actualization. The next logical step. People want to be the best they possibly can be; we want to help them get there.

Conclusion: Money is a motivator—but, as you can see, there're other factors that you can use that will produce positive results.

THE WOODEN PYRAMID
OF SUCCESS

You understand that the Maslow triangle can work with business in particular and people in general, yet you remain skeptical. Fine, let me give you the ultimate proof. It works in sports, where the outcomes have no shades of gray; you either win or lose.

The greatest basketball coach of all time, John Wooden, won ten NCAA national championships (seven in a row) during a twelve-year period, something that was not only unprecedented but may never be repeated. His hierarchy, known as his Pyramid of Success, duplicated Maslow's triangle in many ways.

Seeing this convinced me that Maslow's hierarchy was right.

Go ahead, borrow from the best; I did!

THE ROLE OF REWARDS

I'm a big believer in rewarding people. Are there cash rewards? Some. We pay out bonuses periodically to deserving people. But, as we saw, at a certain point cash is not a huge motivator. Other rewards might include parking closest to the door, a day trip to the spa, a free lunch, or me bringing in a cup of coffee for you.

I don't think you can do this sort of thing enough. You're giving people recognition and bolstering their self-esteem. Sure, you can say, "I pay them; that's enough," but it isn't enough. Take another look at Maslow's triangle to see why.

CASE STUDY: TEAMWORK IN REEL LIFE

Teamwork is a staple in Hollywood movies. It is a constant in war movies and others such as *Aliens*, *Ocean's Eleven*, and *X-Men*. Consider the movie *Twelve O'Clock High*, which was nominated for four Oscars and won two. In 1998, it was selected for preservation by the Library of Congress because it was "culturally, historically, and aesthetically significant."

As that designation would lead you to believe, the film about the U.S. Eighth Air Force's involvement early in World War II is based on a true story. The film stars Gregory Peck as Brigadier General Frank Savage, who takes over the 918th Bomber Group that had been suffering from high losses and a lack of morale and leadership.

Not surprisingly, Savage encounters resistance at first as he tries to improve the unit. Through intensive skill training—and improved discipline—Savage begins to turn around the unit. As the pilots achieve increased success—destroying more enemy targets and suffering fewer losses—they embrace Savage's methods; they become a cohesive, high-performing unit where the pilots and officers feel comfortable offering suggestions that enable the squadron to become even better.

EXERCISE 15: *TWELVE O'CLOCK HIGH*

1. Where do "soft values" such as loyalty, pride, and trust fit in the creation of a high-performing team?

2. When, if at all, do you adjust your leadership style to improve the performance of your team?

3. What is the best way to persuade someone to be part of a team?

4. What do you do if someone refuses to be a good teammate?

5. Will these methods work in today's business world, or only in the movies?

6. Should you copy other successful people, or do what you feel comfortable doing?

SAY THANK YOU

I'm embarrassed to admit that I came to this idea relatively late. I remember on the first day of the Owners/Presidents/Management (OPM) program at Harvard, Marty Marshall, a world-famous mar-

keting professor, got up in front of us and said, "If you don't remember anything else from your time here, remember this: Say
thank you to people who do a good job."

I hadn't been doing it enough, so the moment I got back to the
office I tried it, and I couldn't believe the results. My employees'
faces literally lit up when I said thank you, and their self-esteem
soared.

Because this idea of saying thank you is so important, I will return to it later.

FINDING GOOD TEAMMATES

Clearly, the better the members of the team, the greater the potential for the team to perform well. So you want to absolutely hire the
best people you can. But finding good people takes time. You're
busy, and after you've interviewed the seventh person for a position, there can be the tendency to say, "I've got a million things to
do. They're good enough. Maybe they'll work out; let's go with
them." But if you start to settle for less than the best, your organization will suffer.

Worse, you're giving up a huge potential advantage. There are always going to be people who are smarter than you leading your
competition; and there are always going to be companies that offer
a better product or service than you do. The only way you can narrow those gaps is by having better people than they do. If you settle
during the hiring process, that's never going to happen.

Here is the approach I use to shorten the process of finding great
people. Before you interview with our company, someone has gone
through your background to see if:

1. You have the potential to be a leader. They've looked to see if
you held a leadership position in a previous job or played sports
in school. I look for people who know what it's like to be part of
a team, and who have the potential to be in charge of one.

2. You've demonstrated drive. Maybe you put yourself through college, persuaded your municipality to put in bike lanes, or got your former employer to expand its child-care program. Teams invariably encounter obstacles, and you need to have people who know how to overcome them.

3. You are good with people. This is the hardest one to instantly see from someone's resume, so during an interview I'll ask, "How would you fire someone?"; "A client has called and is complaining about his bill. What would you do?"; or "Let's pretend for a minute that you're interviewing me. What questions would you ask?"

This is only half the battle. You want to hire the best people you can, but you also need to ensure that they're comfortable within your company. If there isn't a good fit, you're not going to get the best out of them.

That's why I'm always extremely candid during the interview process about our company culture. I tell candidates the positives about working for us: how they can move up as fast as their talents allow, the smart and enjoyable people they'll be working with, and that we regularly schedule games and company events to foster friendships and teamwork.

I also tell them what some people consider to be the negatives, such as firing the bottom-performing 10% of our employees every year (after unsuccessful hard work helping to improve their skills). That way, they know that if they are not hard, competent, efficient workers, they probably will want to look somewhere else for a job.

LEARNING FROM OTHERS

I've been fortunate in being able to work with a large number of successful entrepreneurs. Here are some of their ideas and philosophies that have contributed to their successes. You may want to incorporate some of them into your management style. I know I have.

Jay Fitzgerald

Jay is the former president of *Golf Digest* magazine. During his presidency, *Golf Digest* became the number one publication in the golf industry. When I asked Jay if he had any "secrets," he gave me the following ten ideas:

1. Lead by example and set clearly defined goals.
2. Treat everyone—from the maintenance person to the vice president—as equals.
3. Be the voice of the company and set the tone.
4. Keep your "door open," but also walk around the office.
5. Ask for good ideas and stress creativity in all phases of the business.
6. If you find that employees are more interested in vacations, taking all their allocated sick days, asking a lot of questions about their pensions, and constantly late coming in and leaving promptly at 5:00, they are not employees you want to retain. You want employees who pull the wagon, not ride on it.
7. Reward extraordinary performance and establish a winning culture. Do not talk the talk, but back it up by delivering (walk the walk).
8. Pete Carroll, head coach of the Super Bowl–winning Seattle Seahawks, said it very well:
   - Arrive early to meetings.
   - Be prepared.
   - Want to win more than your opponents.
9. Vince Lombardi, famed coach of the Green Bay Packers, said, "Winning isn't everything; it is the only thing."
10. Enjoy what you do and everyone around you will get the message.

Jim Lillie

When Jim arrived to become president of Jarden Industries, a world-class consumer products company with a diverse portfolio of 120 powerful brands like Mr. Coffee, Sunbeam, and Oster, the sales were $300 million. When we did this interview, in 2015 (less than ten years later), sales had risen to $9 billion. So what are Jim's secrets that have contributed to Jarden's incredible growth?

1. Care about your reputation.
2. Conduct your business matters, including the making of acquisitions, in an honest way. Do not be concerned about making the last nickel. Remember that some day you may be involved with the other party again, and you want to have dealt honestly with them the first time.
3. When you make an acquisition, include "earn-outs" as an incentive to the sellers. Also provide a mechanism and tools for the sellers to grow in leadership with the new company.
4. Hire better people than you and develop future leaders.
5. Develop in your management group a "sense that they are owners of the company," not renters. They will care more about the company, just like the owners of homes care more about their houses than renters do.
6. Wear multiple hats and do not be afraid to get your hands dirty.
7. Understand that each new venture starts with a "clean sheet of paper." How you did things before may not work now, because the conditions and facts are different.
8. Know leaders are people who are:
   - Demanding but fair
   - Bold—not afraid to fail
   - Decision makers
   - Good communicators
   - Leaders by example
9. Cultivate leaders, culture:
   - Hire for values.
   - Share information.

- Encourages a lot of new thinking.
- Do your job.

10. Hold meetings when needed. The CEO sets the time and is not a traffic cop, but more a facilitator.

THE WILL TO MAKE THE IMPOSSIBLE POSSIBLE

We talked about Hess Oil earlier, but this story fits best here.

In the 1980s, Leon Hess decided to build a 40,000-barrel/day refinery to produce fuel in St. Croix, U.S. Virgin Islands.

The average time to complete a similar refinery, including infrastructure, was over two years. Hess decided it could be done in six months.

So almost every Friday for six months, he flew from New Jersey to the refinery construction site in St. Croix and held a meeting with all the key people involved in the project. Leon sat with them around a large table in a trailer. Each person at the table reported where he or she was at in the project, whether it was on schedule or whether there was anything that could occur to delay the project.

All items were put on the table and resolved right then.

The bottom line: the refinery was up and running in six months.

Nick Trigony

Nick was president of Cox Broadcasting, an executive at ABC and Blair Radio, and excelled at all three companies. His thoughts about being successful:

1. Do not be afraid to fail.

2. Set an example for everyone else.

3. Give credit for success to others, but take responsibility for failures.

4. Surround yourself with the best people you can. Find smart, honest, hardworking people—no jerks or "yes" people.

5. Empower people by giving them leeway, flexibility, and the ability to make decisions.

6. Have people bring you their problems, but ask them to also bring recommended solutions.

7. Build up trust. Be a person of your word.

8. Have your team's input when setting goals, but also challenge them to grow the company and exceed expectations.

9. You know you've established the right culture if people want to come to work.

10. Understand that not everyone can lead or want to lead.

11. Manage up and down the chain of command.

12. Be sure your spouse and family support you. I changed jobs and moved several times in my career.

13. When the economy goes bad, stay the course and be more innovative.

14. Work in an honest way with competitors and people you report to. You never know when they can help you in the future.

Tom Quinlan

Tom is president and CEO of the NASDAQ-listed company RR Donnelley. It is the largest provider of printing and print-related business in the world and has over 65,000 employees and revenue of approximately $12 billion. I asked him about his management style and the secrets of his success. Here's what he told me:

1. Reward performance. The reward does not always have to be monetary.

2. Do not ask people to do things you are not willing to do.

3. Make decisions. Make the tough decisions as soon as possible.

4. Communicate, communicate, and communicate. Keep e-mails to twenty-five words or less. Any e-mails greater than twenty-five words, pick up the phone and call the person.

5. Do not get complacent. Continue to evolve both yourself and your business.

6. Realize that great progress is made when you check your ego at the door.

7. Be polite and courteous; say, "Thank you."

Bob McLynn

Bob is co-founder and owner of Crush Music. He is the business manager for some of the most popular musical acts in the United States, with clients such as Train and Fall Out Boy. You will see in his answers to "What made you successful?" that it is all about expertise, hard work, passion, teamwork, and being a calculated risk-taker.

His answers:

1. I set a time limit (age thirty) to either make it as an artist or go into something else.

2. I understand the business I am in. My partner Jonathan Daniel and I started as musicians and toured the country. Managing bands was a natural extension and, with our background, gave us a competitive advantage. We felt we were artists working with other artists.

3. When we recognized a talented band, we gave them the benefit of our expertise and even in some cases provided them with financial support.

4. We really enjoy our profession. It is essential because there are times we work eighty-hour weeks.

FOUR TAKEAWAYS FROM THIS CHAPTER

1. **If you want to grow and succeed,** build an effective team. There is no other way.

2. **Give credit for success to others, but take responsibility for failures.** People need to trust that you're not going to ridicule their ideas. They should know that if their idea doesn't work, it isn't their fault, it's yours.

3. **Remember, the most effective way to build a team** is through face-to-face communication.

4. **Reread the list of comments at the end of the chapter** from the CEOs interviewed, and adapt the advice and techniques to your style.

Give Back

I was going to make this chapter part of another one, but I think the underlying idea is too important.

As you go through life, you don't merely want to be good—good at what you do for a living; good as a person; good to your family, friends, and community—you want to be great. And, part of being great is helping people.

You have to give back.

When I say that, some people wonder why they have to. They tell me they obey all laws, pay their taxes, and vote. They take care of their families and they're good neighbors. Isn't that enough, they ask.

No.

You really do want to treat people the way you would like them to treat you. If you needed some help, you would like someone to provide it. What naturally follows is that you should be willing to help others in need. What comes with success is a responsibility to help those who have not been as fortunate.

In fact, I believe that responsibility starts even before you're truly successful. I encourage people to begin giving back as early as possible. With our kids, we tied the concept to their bar and bat mitzvahs; 10% of what they received in gifts, they donated to the charity of their choice. This is how engrained the idea is for Lois and me.

Now, you don't have to start quite that early, but I do think you should be giving back the moment you have a job. Why? Well, one reason, I believe, is because this is an important thing to do. And for another, I don't think this is something you can—or should—put off, to where you only give when things are going well for you. No, you want to get into the habit of helping people early on, and stay in this habit throughout your life.

Everyone has a responsibility to give back.

I know younger people are going to object when I say they should be giving back from day one of their working life. After all, when you're just starting out, money is tight. (It certainly was for me.)

If my suggestion, giving back from the day you receive your first paycheck, is going to make you cranky, then this is going to make you livid: I think everyone should give 10% of what they make— and they should be contributing that amount from day one as well.

In the Hebrew Torah there is a concept called Maaser. It's a three-year cycle. In year 1, 10% was given to the high priests. In year 2, 10% was given to the Levite Group who performed religious acts. In year 3, 10% was given to the poor and orphans. And then the cycle was repeated. This concept in other religions is called tithing. Even if you're not religious, I advise you do this.

Now, let me be quick to stress that the 10% does not have to be in cash. You can give your time, goods, or services in addition to (or instead of) cash. How you give is negotiable, but how much is not.

Where or to whom do you give? This is a personal decision. However, typically you're going to feel better about giving to a charity you have a connection to.

Let me give you some quick examples.

I have always given to cancer research; but when I was diagnosed with cancer, giving back became more personal for me. I started working directly with the Dana-Farber Cancer Institute in Boston, a world leader in adult and pediatric cancer treatment and research, to help them with their fund-raising. I am very lucky to have received wonderful and effective care during my treatment, and I want to be a part of giving back to help others in similar circumstances.

Conversely, people who have taken their children to a local hospital and received good treatment and services may choose to fund the local children's hospital.

You think your local religious facility should have a nursery so young parents can attend services, instead of being forced to stay home with their kids. Everyone agrees, but says there is no money, so you start a fund-raising effort on your own.

Do you feel you received a good college education that helped you to be successful? I donate to my alma maters, Harvard and Rutgers. I also contribute to Babson because I think the education Babson provides is stellar and so important. *Money* magazine and *U.S. News & World Report* have, for many years, named Babson the best college in America for entrepreneurship. It is a real privilege to have taught there for over fifteen years.

If you want to remember those who gave their lives on September 11, there are a number of charities you can contribute to, including one that my family supports, Jeremy's Heroes.

Do something that makes sense for you.

Should you be strategic? If you do business with golfers, should you fund golf-related charities? Well, I'm neutral on this issue. Whether you like it or not, that is probably going to end up happening. If you serve as a senior manager for a company, and the CEO has a charity that he's particularly fond of, you're probably going to end up making a contribution. It's just another example of funding something that's important to you; that is, staying in the boss's good graces.

It's just human nature; most people find it easier to reach for their checkbook if they can relate to the charity.

That, by the way, is also the way you get people to give if you're in charge of fund-raising. You need to connect the cause, issue, or project you are trying to raise money for to something that's important to the people you're asking to contribute. Sure, you can simply ask them for money, but if you tie your request to something they care about, your odds of receiving a donation go up substantially. (You can see how this easily ties to the top two layers of Maslow's hierarchy of needs—esteem and self-actualization.)

Here's an example. You're trying to raise money for athletic facilities in your town. You could knock on doors at random and ask for a contribution. Or you could figure out who are the richest, most generous people in town, and try to determine what they will respond to.

Giving back is simply good karma.

Well, in this case, not surprisingly, people who care about sports are more likely to give. You find that one of the people in town is a fanatical follower of the local college football team. Could you arrange for him to have lunch, or, better yet, play a round of golf with the head coach in the off-season? If you could, your odds of receiving an extremely large check would go up dramatically.

If they have children who have played in school sports or are currently involved, they make great candidates as well.

My friend Pat Boyle is a very successful entrepreneur. After he sold one of his companies, he was able to spend more time at home with his kids. Like Pat, they were athletes. One problem, he found, was that the football and baseball fields did not have stadium lights, so this limited the use of the facilities.

Pat spent three years holding many fund-raisers and attending zoning meetings to work through any challenges they faced so the fields could have lights. They now enjoy evening games and practices, thanks to his efforts.

Cenveo chairman Bob Burton admits that he would not have gone to college unless he had received a football scholarship. So, he founded the Cenveo scholarship program for children of Cenveo employees. They've raised $2 million so far.

The connection makes all the difference.

OTHER EXAMPLES

Just as only you can decide what ethical standards you're going to adopt, only you can decide how, if at all, you want to try to capitalize on your ethical behavior.

Target, for example, has a sign in every one of its stores saying it gives 5% of profits to local charities, going so far as to break down how much it's given to each nearby town. At Blue Buffalo, we have the Buff Foundation that funds dog and cat cancer research. Our contributions are based on sales. You can see on our website that we give millions each year.

You need to do what feels right and comfortable for you. Ultimately, you're the one who has to decide whether you are going to be a mensch or not.

PEER PRESSURE 101

Here's something else I have learned about giving, and it struck me as counterintuitive. For the longest time, I was more than happy to give and to receive no credit for doing so. People would offer to put up a plaque in my honor, or name something after me, and every time I said no. "I'm just happy to give," I said. "I don't want any recognition."

Well, President Len Schlesinger, who brought me to Babson when he was head of the college, told me, in no uncertain terms, that my modesty was a bad idea.

"If I can put your name on something, I can go to your wealthier friends and colleagues and say, 'You see what Len Green contributed? You have a lot more money than he does, what are you going to fund?'"

It's a very clever approach. People are naturally competitive and they're going to want to outdo whatever their friends and colleagues have done. Of course, the charity benefits as a result.

A variation on this can work on a far smaller scale. For example, invariably our employees' kids are involved in some sort of fund-raising venture. The local Girl Scout troop wants to go on a trip; the swim team needs money to be able to compete at a regional event.

I always tell the parents to put the cookies, wrapping paper, or magazine gift subscription the kids are selling on our receptionist's desk so the other employees can see it when they walk in. I also suggest something else. I tell them to leave a contribution sheet there as well, so everyone can see who made the purchases (and can figure out who didn't). I try to be the first person to sign up. You'd be amazed at how effective this approach is in increasing contributions.

I don't care what it takes to get you to give. I only care that you do.

ONE FINAL NOTE: THE PROFITS FROM THIS BOOK

I sincerely hope you have taken from this book a few ideas that will make you more successful.

All profits from this book will be contributed to charity. It's called putting my money where my mouth is.

Thank you for reading.

Say Thank You

As we have seen, you cannot say thank you enough. That is certainly true in my case.

GRATITUDE TO MY TEAM

Let me introduce you to my team, past and present. Without them, I could never have achieved my success.

My wife, Lois Green, has been my boss and my "right hand in everything" for over fifty-seven years. She is the true reason for any success I have achieved.

My daughter Beth Green, a lawyer who has consulted for me on many Babson case studies and business matters.

My daughter Debra Green, a lawyer and president of the Jeremy's Heroes Foundation, has been my adviser in legal, personal, and business matters for over fifteen years.

My son, Jonathan Green, Targeted Financial Services partner, has advised me in finances, advertising, the horses, and strategy for over ten years.

Karlene Bauer, director of administration and operations at The Green Group, manages the real estate division, and has given me incredible advice and feedback for over thirty years.

Jim Benkoil, CPA, CVA, and Frank Palino, EA, CDFA, ATA, have been partners in The Green Group for over twenty years.

Kathy Anderson was a great mentor for over twenty years before she left to start a very successful brokerage and financial company.

Les Charm, professor at Babson College, has been a true friend and consultant for over fifteen years.

Kate Paynter left to become a successful hospitality manager with a catering and banquet company, over ten years.

Dianne Sellmeyer has been a secretary and administrator in taxes, real estate, and in my horse business for over thirty years.

Donna Tumminia, my assistant, formerly worked with senior management at AIG, over ten years.

Donna Tumulty left to work with her husband in the money management field, over ten years.

Marianne Velcamp, CPA and consultant, over twenty years.

Michael Panitch, VP of Smith Barney, has been a friend and a counselor of mine for over twenty-five years.

Rabbi Arnold Lasker taught me to always be prepared for any question.

Rabbi Jack Rosoff for his guidance.

The other members of my family, Honi Robins, Michelle Green, and Marty Feinberg.

Ellen Kadin, executive editor, AMACOM Books.

Joe Scutellaro—a former partner who was always there for me.

My parents, Abe and Helen Green, for their guidance and love.

John Altman, a teacher, mentor, and humanitarian, my best friend and business adviser for over thirty years.

Acknowledgments

The standard procedure in this section is to say thanks and give an acknowledgement to my wife Lois, my family, co-workers and clients who have contributed their input to this book.

Since I have done that elsewhere, I would also like to acknowledge the great advice I have received from the people I have met and gotten to know. I truly have been blessed with mentors and friends who have helped me along the way.

I have included some of these people in this book, but I am sure I left out or greatly short-changed others. Believe me, it was not intentional. And if I did not include you on the page, please know I will always remember you and your words and I greatly appreciate it.

Over my lifetime I have read about and worked with many successful entrepreneurs. In my opinion, one of the greatest was Steve Jobs, co-founder, chairman and CEO of Apple.

In the late 1990's, Apple branded itself with the famously grammatically questionable tagline "Think Different." The capstone of the campaign was a TV commercial known as "Here's to the Crazy Ones."

As images of iconic activists, artists, explorers and scientists flashed on the screen, the following words were recited.

"Here's to the crazy ones. The misfits. The rebels. The troublemakers. The round pegs in square holes. The ones who see things differently. They're not fond of rules. And they have no respect for the status quo. You can quote them, disagree with them, glorify or vilify them. About the only thing you can't do is ignore them. Because they change things. They push the human race forward. And while some may see them as the crazy ones, we see genius. Because the people who are crazy enough to think they can change the world, are the ones who do."

I encourage you to change the world.

Thank you again for reading.

MY STUDY GROUP

Let me tell you a little bit about members of my study group at the Harvard Business School OPM program.

Dr. John Altman, a Protestant minister who ran a successful plastics company, was elected president of the class. John grew up on the South Side of Chicago and worked summers at the country club, where he was paid solely in tips. He learned to hustle and give his customers fast, efficient, and courteous service. In return, he was one of the club's most respected and rewarded employees. He later went to Miami of Ohio and played football.

Geoff Murphy was from Australia and started working in construction while in high school. He possessed a great work ethic and within a few years became owner of the company. Geoff had an uncanny ability to find solutions to cases that came from his drive to succeed. Geoff was not limited in his thinking by what they taught in college—because he never went there. By the end of the three-year class, Geoff's construction company was the largest in Australia/New Zealand.

Andreas Schweitzer was from Switzerland, and all we knew about him was that he was from a family business in the hotel industry. In the first year of OPM, as a joke, we would leave our dirty laundry next to his door. He never objected. He was quiet but spoke with a lot of wisdom.

When we came back the second year, we each found a brochure next to our door that announced that the hotel he ran, the Dolder Grand

Hotel in Zurich, Switzerland, had been voted the number one hotel in the world based on value and service. Boy, were we embarrassed!

Jay McCabe, an attorney from Boston, had been the head of logistics for Gillette. He then decided to start his own logistics company and came to the OPM program. His company's strengths included: knowledge of the industry, better personal service (twenty-four/seven), and continuous innovation to solve present and future problems. We were surprised by how many large companies utilized him for his motivational expertise, in addition to hiring him for their logistics work.

Phillip Stein, the youngest member of our group, was from California and had an MBA from Berkeley. He was the only member of the group who was computer-savvy, and he had a lot of business experience with family businesses in the retail trade. Though he's had over a dozen eye operations, he keeps working.

For one year, Carlos Mattos was part of our group. He was from Colombia, in South America; smart as a whip; and enjoyed his social life very much. We wondered if he would ever be successful. When I was elected to the Babson Board of Trustees in 2013, Carlos was one of the board members. By that time, he was owner and CEO of over a hundred car dealerships in Colombia.

Index